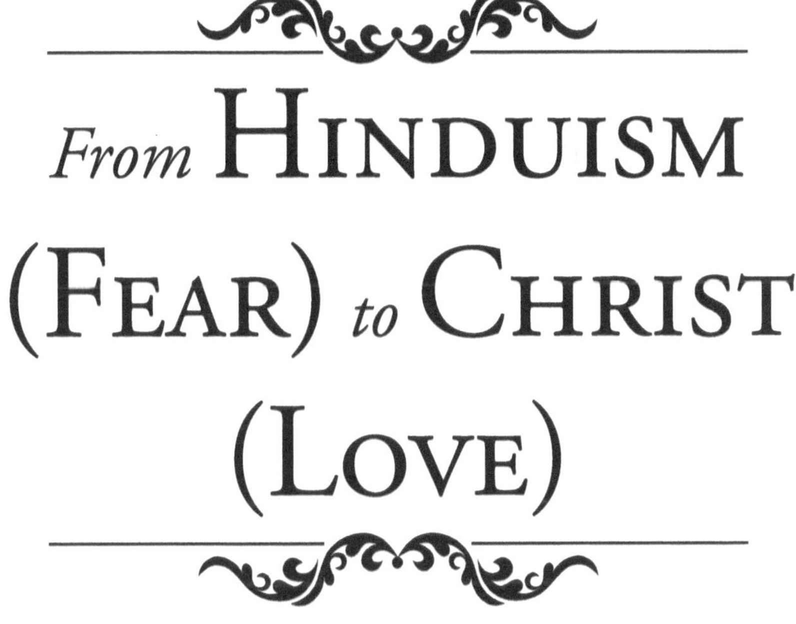

From HINDUISM (FEAR) *to* CHRIST (LOVE)

Renewing the Mind: A Transformative Journey as a First-Generation Christian and American

Jonali Bulsiewicz

ISBN 979-8-88540-123-4 (paperback)
ISBN 979-8-88616-940-9 (hardcover)
ISBN 979-8-88540-124-1 (digital)

Christian Faith Publishing
832 Park Avenue
Meadville, PA 16335
www.christianfaithpublishing.com

Printed in the United States of America

To God. It was His idea, and I had many doubts that this book would go anywhere because I don't have a "name," but He has given me the highest of names: a daughter of a King. Thank You, for bringing me out of the depths into glory. You have been so patient with me, and I've settled, once and for all, that I cannot live or function without You.

To Timothy, my faithful husband whom I don't deserve. Your love for me has been so steadfast, and being married to my best friend for over a decade has been the best answer to prayer in my life. Thank you for your love and support.

To my children, Elijah and Priya. God used you to help me fight for my life when you were a baby and toddler. Thank you for being flexible, for being leaders, and for your childlike faith that inspires me every day. I have one of the best jobs in the world: to raise you both to be world changers!

Preface

My heart's cry for this book is to relay a message of hope to the hopeless, to bring light to the darkest of circumstances, to write about a love that triumphs fear, and most importantly, to express the *abundant life* in obedience and surrender unto the Author of the universe.

Disclaimer: To any Hindus reading this book, I pray you read it with an open mind. An amazing truth is that God loves us so much that He gives us free will to choose Him. It's not His nature nor character to force Himself on us.

Chapter 1

THE BLIND YEARS

My parents were born and raised in India. My dad was a double refugee from Burma and Bangladesh but grew up in Calcutta (Kolkata). My mom was from a royal family from Tripura, which is in the easternmost part of India. I am a distant relative of R. D. and S. D. Burman who were some of the most famous musicians in India. If you ask anyone a bit older in India, they would definitely have heard of them. My cousin is one of the first females to have a stamp after her in the state of Tripura and a well-known musician. There are writers, musicians, and photographers in my family, so it seems like our bloodline has a gift with the arts. My parents were in an arranged marriage and are a decade apart in age. In Indian culture, we call it a love marriage or an arranged marriage. Although the popularity of arranged marriages in India is decreasing, it still exists today. Like most immigrants back in the years of the 1960s, if they are educated enough, they would move to America or any Westernized nation to look for work and raise a family. Unbeknown to them, my parents were pioneers at heart. They met and, a few weeks later, were married (1972). And a few weeks after that, they left their home, family, and the land of their ancestors to have a better life in a foreign country.

My dad worked a few different jobs in the beginning of their years in America, and my mom gave birth to my sister, Piyali, and I while her family was oceans away. When I was about to start school, we settled in upstate New York in Albany, a couple of hours north of New York City. As I began school, I realized that I had a different skin color than my peers and was embarrassed when my parents would speak in their native tongue, Bengali, in front of others. My culture taught me that the fairer skin I had, the more beautiful I was; so the insecurity of being dark-skinned birthed at a young age. I believed this lie in my early childhood years and would do anything to stay out of the sun so that I wouldn't get darker. I started to become ashamed of my culture and wished I was born with white skin as I wanted to look the same as everyone else. It was sort of ingrained in me to care about what others think on the outside. I started to understand that my White friends had different rules, ate different food, and were different from me in numerous ways. I felt like I was an outsider, not only because of my skin color but because of all the differences culturally. I learned that I was something called an ABCD (American-born confused desi). This is a term that refers to first-generation South Asians who are born in the United States and are disconnected with the culture of their parents and ancestors. They are classified as confused because they grow up mixed between their parents' and American culture. I also believed, from Indian culture, that my parents wanted a son. Culturally, sons become providers for their parents. And because I was the second born, and they already had a daughter, I felt rejected, worthless, and invaluable.

I grew up going to the temple and worshipping idols. There were statues all around the holy room where the smell of incense and fruit baskets would awaken my sense of smell. There was money at the foot of these statues as well. I knew there was a god for everything, and I would worship the one that was specific to my need. For example, I would worship Lakshmi if I wanted wealth or Saraswati for knowledge. In my mind, I was trying to earn acceptance with my own strength. Fear of not worshipping correctly or doing something bad would hinder how these gods approved my lifestyle. I also wanted to please my parents to win their love and acceptance. According to the belief of reincarnation, if I wasn't good in this life, I would pay for it in the next one by being regenerated into something bad. My life slowly became paralyzed with fear. I was allowing fear into my life, not only by believing lies but by opening myself up to spirits that, at the time, I didn't realize were wrong. We weren't allowed to wear shoes into the temple. I remember one time I did and was scolded, and my friend said, "Your shoes have entered a place no shoes have ever been." Shoes are considered dirty from the road and also are sometimes made from leather, which derived from dead animals. I also remember, when it was a certain time of the month, I wasn't allowed to enter the room where all the gods were because it was considered dirty. Between the fear, the pressure, potentially upsetting different gods, the what ifs, possibly upsetting my family, social pressure, and confusion, anxiety began to overwhelm me.

My sister was also smart as she did well in school and had amazing talents, like singing, dancing, and writing. My parents, naturally, would always rave about her, and she was my hero since I didn't have the same talents. I lived under her shadow and was known to others as "Piyali's sister." As I came into my high school years, the insecurity of being Indian came back to haunt me and only worsened since I went to a mostly White high school. Being insecure, I always wondered if people would look at me funny because I was a minority or believed teachers would treat me differently because I had darker skin. These were all lies, but they seemed true inside my mind. I also remember waking up pretty early to make myself look "hot" as I started to seek attention from boys. I began to go down the path of getting a "look" from a desirable boy. When I started to get a few looks, this made me crave them even more. It actually became like an addiction. I made sure of going to the gym every day to try and look like the models I had seen on TV or in magazines. Thankfully, social media wasn't big yet, so it was more just looking great during school then coming home and changing back into sweat pants, like it was all a facade. I started to go to parties at neighboring high schools to meet new men for new highs. I had an early curfew, so I would wait until my parents would go to bed and sneak out. I remember sneaking out to go to a boy's house, and on the way home, my car got stuck in snow, so I found myself digging my car out in sandals in the middle of winter and getting frostbite. Somehow, I managed to hide that, and thankfully, my toes are still on my feet today. I then lied to my parents, saying I dropped something in the snow, and it took a while to find it. Lying became so normal to me in my teenage years, to the point where I wouldn't think twice about it. I was like a hamster on a wheel going in circles. I remember traveling to France during my senior year and really loving getting attention from boys, especially the Native French ones. Listening to the lies of the enemy, they were more attractive because they spoke a beautiful language. Flirting was an endless, empty cycle of trying to get attention. I've heard it being phrased as "licking each other's wounds." Trying to put a Band-Aid on deep wounds that lasted for years. And guys were where I felt most accepted on the outside, only to find myself more depressed on the inside.

My senior year of high school came around, and my sister came home from university for the spring holiday with some incredible news. With a glow in her eyes, she shared with me that she had found God. I wasn't shocked when she told me this news. I saw something dramatically different in her. She was a completely new person. There was a transformation. She proceeded to tell me that she felt empty at a college party and, in desperation, left the party. Outside in a snowy field, she cried out to God, exclaiming that she wanted more. To her (unexpected) surprise, He lovingly revealed Himself to her in a tangible way and responded to her plea. With an open heart, I was so excited for my sister as she finally seemed satisfied and full of joy. Her words didn't have an impact on me, but her transformed life did. In the week she was home, she was a completely different person. I started to question everything. Is this God real? Is there only one God? Is there only one truth? What happens after I die? Is there truly a God out there that loves us *unconditionally*, and I don't have to do anything to earn it? If there is, then I want *that* God.

I was lifeguarding with my Christian friend at the time and began to ask him these questions. At the time, he thought he was just answering my questions, but the Holy Spirit used him to answer those questions exactly the way my heart needed to hear them. My search for God began. He then invited me to a youth group where there was worship and a message. I was completely shocked at the sincerity of these Christians as they lifted their hands to worship their

God. They weren't trying to put on a show or doing it out of obligation; but instead, it was genuine. I started to weep uncontrollably. Being shy at the time, I tried to hold back the tears with all of my might, but I failed. There was something to this God, and I wanted what these Christians had. As the night was coming to a close, I asked the youth leader some more questions about God. Again, every answer was perfect. I remember the drive home as it was snowing hard. Everything seemed to be so pure and peaceful. Every streetlight seemed to be shining directly at me. I knew I couldn't wait any longer to give my life to Jesus.

I got home and went directly to my room. The presence of God was heavy all around me. I didn't understand what was happening. It was like I was being pulled by a loving force I knew I wanted to submit to. I told God I was sorry for everything that I did and that I wanted Him to be my Father. I didn't want to live for myself anymore but instead to please Him. The prayer was simple and to the point. When I opened my eyes, I felt an overwhelming peace I had never experienced before. It seemed as if I had been blind my entire life, up until this moment. Now I could finally see clearly. The best part of opening my eyes was I finally felt satisfied and full. I was truly born again in the sense that I felt a new person. I immediately tore down posters of boy models and materialistic labels that were all over my walls. I didn't know why at the time, but I realized I didn't want anything to do with that anymore. I felt like I was on cloud nine and starting life all over again. I had joy, peace, and love straight away, something I never had before.

Chapter 2

TEMPTATIONS AND PERSECUTION

I knew that I had to keep my newfound relationship with God to myself. My sister had told my parents right away, but the fear that was inside me was not ready to tell them. Thankfully, I was months away from going to university. In the short time between the end of high school and college, I had a few loving Christians in my life. However, I did not seek out discipleship in a sense of regular mentoring, nor did I know what accountability was at the time. I was a new Christian and didn't know how crucial discipleship was. I didn't have a church to go to either. I didn't know there were certain things I should have done to build my faith, like reading the word or worshipping or even spending time with Him. All I knew was, now I have God in me. Life seems different, and I have a lot more conviction in my life than I once did.

Because of my lack of realizing many things as a new believer, I started to get distracted by getting attention from guys once again as I had not been healed of some deeper wounds from my childhood. It was almost as if the pull to getting attention from guys was even stronger than it was before I said "yes" to Jesus. Looking back, I realize how much Satan just wanted me to be the seed that withered because it had no root. Of course, he is ruthless and is going to attack a helpless new Christian that has no foundation over a mature, believing one. It's almost as if I had this special thing about me where guys really started to notice me even more. It was a complete lie I had believed at the time; but unfortunately, I had no idea I was even listening to a demonic voice and fell for almost anything he would throw at me. When I was out of my parents' home in university, I used the freedom for more rebellion. I loved having no rules or curfews and not having to answer to anyone about the time I got home. I had freedom on the outside but was really a prisoner on the inside. I was not a fan of my parents' strict rules, especially since my American friends did not have the same rules. Now I was trying to live a double life where I would party on the weekends but still be involved with the Christian group on campus during the week. I had a conviction about the way that I was living, but I constantly ignored it until my conscience was seared. I loved the world and what it had to offer more than God because it was temporary pleasure, and I was still into myself. I gave my life to Jesus on March 17, 2001 but didn't realize that I had to die daily and transform. My conscience became so seared that I started to date someone who was not a Christian. The pull for flesh and getting attention from a guy appeared so much stronger than God at the time, and I was completely giving into Satan's plan for my life: to destroy me and pull me away from God. I knew that it was wrong the whole time but did not have the strength to break if off with him.

For an entire year, I turned my back on God, thinking that I knew better or just liking the attention from a man. After all, he was my first boyfriend, and I wanted to prove to someone that a White man could be attracted to an Indian girl. I continued to keep striving, ignored my convictions, and transferred to a better university to play division 1 tennis. I was an emotional mess, going from one thing to the next, phasing for the tennis team, going to parties, dating, trying to be accepted with the girls in the team, struggling academically since this university was harder. I also had to try and hide this from my parents because they were so proud of me going to a good school, and I didn't want to disappoint them at all. After a semester of struggling there, I transferred back to my old university.

My parents weren't happy and didn't understand. I transferred back not only because that was where my boyfriend was but because something inside of me knew I had to. I returned for the spring semester, living with my friends who I had once partied with. Slowly, I began to stop going to parties and got more involved with the Christian group and church. I realized I could not live this double life anymore and had to choose a side. All my Christian friends were telling me to break up with my boyfriend, but I would ignore them out of complete pride.

My Pastor, at the time, decided to do water baptisms. I had never been baptized when God found me, so I took this opportunity. I remember coming out of that water feeling new and clean from all the iniquity. The conviction of my boyfriend only got stronger. It came to a point where I couldn't ignore it anymore and had to make a hard decision. It was around May when the semester ended, and I went home for the summer. I called him, and it seemed like I literally lost control of my mouth because I said, "I can't do this anymore. I am sorry." I had no intention of breaking up with him that day, but it was almost as if God knew I didn't have the strength; and out of His love for me, He did it on my behalf. It was almost as if He took over my mouth and tongue. He knew that my heart wanted to, but my head was getting in the way. I hung up the phone in shock but felt a peace overwhelmed me, the same peace that I had when I first accepted God into my life. My sister also told me to write a list of everything I wanted in a future husband. I made a list of about thirty characteristics and then put it away. This helped me to also realize that he was nothing that I wanted in a future husband because the first thing I wrote on that list was "a man who loves God with all of his heart." This was the first time I had been in willful obedience for an entire year of my life, but I was so grateful as when I actually obeyed, God forgave me and was willing to give me another chance.

A few days after this, and still being in some emotional pain from breaking up with my boyfriend, I felt another conviction that I never really had before. Out of nowhere, I heard the Holy Spirit whisper, "Why are you lying about Me to your parents?" What? This was completely out of nowhere as I never really felt bad about it before.

In that moment, I stopped everything I was doing and realized that for two years, I had been telling my parents I wasn't a Christian. They suspected this after my sister became a Christian and thought she tried to convert me. Although I gave my life to God shortly after her, I had lied about it when they asked me if I was a Christian. I wrestled with God, thinking it was only May. I didn't go back to school until late August. I could lie for just three more months and tell them just before I go back to university. That way, I could tell them and then run off. I started trying to ignore God but began to lose my appetite, not able to sleep. I would sometimes even feel nauseated from ignoring the conviction. Having just recovered from finally giving up my boyfriend, I knew I could not ignore Him yet again with another area of my life. It was so strong to the point where I knew I had to tell my parents. I called on my pastor and his wife and asked if I could go to their house and explain the situation to them. They prayed for me and reassured me it was going to be okay. They would support me in whatever way they were able. The next time my parents asked me, I was ready to tell them. I was at a friend's house, and I received a phone call. My dad asked me again, "Jonali, are you a Christian?" With my heart pounding, I replied, "Yes, Daddy, I am." He hung up. I was so scared to go home but had nowhere else to go. I cried and prayed. I came home to my dad's angry face and his expressing words from a place of hurt. It was late, so I just went up to my room in complete fear and anticipation of what the next few days were going to look like.

They, of course, were hurt, angry, confused, and didn't understand why I had also become a Christian. They figured they lost my sister, in a sense, and now they were going to lose me. It felt like a taste of martyrdom, even though they never threatened my life. There was nothing in me that could deny Him. He was real, and He had changed my life. There was no going back to the old life full of sin and apart from God. Every day, for that entire summer, I was faced with a lot of reaction based out of complete hurt. I cried every day, but the peace I had from obeying God outweighed the earthly circumstances. I would turn to the Bible and read Psalm 27:10, knowing that I would be okay. I would literally feel God's tangible presence around me when everything else seemed to be in complete disarray. The persecution only made my faith stronger. It was the first test to see whether or not I would deny Him in a tough situation. The peace was so strong; and at the time, the attack was heavy. But the more I spent time with my Father (mostly crying in His arms), it would give me the strength I needed to go through those three months. I was only a few years old in the Lord, and He was so gracious to be there for me. With God, I was accelerated in the depth of my faith. It was like getting a large promotion at work quickly in a new job. The "promotion" wasn't anything that was seen; it was hidden in my heart and something that, one day, I will get rewarded for in heaven, according to His word. Persecution in the church today is growing rapidly, and I honor those with all of my heart that have been killed for their faith. I've found that where there is persecution, usually, there is multiplication and revival as well.

Without going to God first during those three months, I would have lost my mind and maybe even been suicidal. Looking back, I am actually so glad that I didn't really have a Christian community to help me through this. I didn't have people calling to tell me that "it was going to be okay." Nor did I have people to run to out of the despair and complete brokenness. I had Jesus, and Jesus alone. He is the only one that has the capacity to heal the most broken places, and the beautiful thing is that we can fully trust Him. Neither did I have thoughts of, *If God loved me, why would He do this to me?* or *Life should be easy when we are in Christ.* It was, in fact, the opposite. God didn't cause my parents to get upset with me or do anything bad to me. He said in James chapter 1 that we would have trials.

I believe Satan only goes harder when we fully submit and surrender to Him. I submitted to Him first and knew the result wasn't going to be pretty. I knew God loved me, having established that in my heart; and I wanted to do what was right before Him. Lying wasn't an option anymore, and I was surprised I was so comfortable in that for a time period. There is a reason why Christians are being martyred for their faith. They usually have the choice to deny that God is real in order to not get killed. But in their hardest of hearts, they can't because He has been too real to them. Once you experience

Him personally and regularly, there is absolutely no going back. It is virtually impossible. I am so thankful for the persecution I went through. It made me pray for my parents more, forgive them more, and love them more. It also helped me to get ready for the persecution I would face from friends and people in the future. It set me up for victory in loving those who hate me, forgiving those who hurt me, and turning the other cheek. It helped me to not take things personally and learn that, usually, people don't mean what they say.

Words are powerful, and I was so sensitive to them. But in Christ, and in my weakness, He was strong. "My grace is sufficient for you, for my power is made perfect in weakness." Therefore, I will boast all the more gladly about my weakness so that Christ's power may rest on me. That is why, for Christ's sake, I delight in weaknesses, in insults, in hardships, in persecutions, in difficulties. For when I am weak, then I am strong (2 Corinthians 12:9–11). I would not have made it through this if it wasn't for God literally holding me every night. The power came in my submission to Him and His lordship over my life. If I wasn't humbled by all the brokenness and thought for one second that I could go through that in my own strength, I would have fallen right away and told God that "I was done with Him.

Sometimes we need brokenness in our lives for humility so that pride has no place. Breaking up with a man after a year of dating and going through hardship with my parents was the perfect storm for me to not have an ounce of myself left at the time. We have two choices always in a time of brokenness. We can either go to the Healer (Jesus) directly, or we can go to temporary highs, like friendships, spouses, food, drink, substances, television, social media, video games, work, etc.—basically, anything other than Christ. The problem is, only God can heal and give solutions to problems. Is it okay to get godly counsel sometimes? Of course. But I believe that we need to always go to Jesus first before any pastor or anyone in a leadership position because we get more dependent on a person than Jesus Himself. For some reason, it seems easier to go to solutions in the flesh rather than being in the prayer closet. The battle can only truly be won in the prayer closet and in Christ. Spending time with

Jesus is the absolute best medicine we can ever take. We always are better off after spending time with Him and allowing Him to speak to our hearts. If we are having a hard time questioning His voice, we always have His word, and He often speaks through it. Our souls will never get sick if we keep drinking from the life that only He can give!

Chapter 3

POWER OF SURRENDER

I went back to university in my junior year full of faith (and armor). Now that I didn't have a boyfriend holding me back and just been through extreme testing of my faith with persecution on the home front, I was ready to tell everybody about Jesus and not care what anyone else would say or think. There was an extreme power there that came from full obedience and surrender. I was given a position of being an RA (resident assistant) on the basement floor of our dormitory, in charge of the girls on my floor, and had to do different duties throughout that year. Everyone knew that I was a Christian and did not like it. I would get comments left and right of how brainwashed I was and that I was a "Jesus freak." Because of what I had gone through earlier, none of these comments fazed me. It was as though He trained me for not allowing hurtful words to have an effect on me. I was so in love with Jesus that all I cared about was what He said about me. If we truly believe what the word says about us, no other words should affect us as they are more than powerful. If anything, the hurtful words made me stronger in my faith, and God used it as a time to help me to love and pray for my enemies. He was still sharpening me and helping me to keep my heart pure through the attack. This was a beautiful semester as I was fully surrendered to the Lord and became a leader in my Christian group as well. I wasn't living that double life anymore and had no shame or guilt. I was completely free from the sin that once held me and was much quicker to repent for sin than I was before. With nothing holding me back, I was like a bird—finally free, out of a cage that I had been trapped in. I was pursuing God with everything in me, and He would pursue me. My dorm was beside a beautiful lake called Lake Ontario. I had many quiet times with Him sitting on the rocks, praying, reading the word, and allowing Him to speak to me. He helped me develop a solid relationship with Him. He would father me and woo me every single day. I would talk to Him on the way to class and just fell in love with the Creator who first fell in love with me. I remember doing better in school as well. Life finally seemed like I was thriving, not just surviving.

When I went home for the Christmas holiday, it wasn't as hard, or maybe they were; but because in Christ, words did not affect me. My best friend, who I had met a few years ago, was now at a local YMCA. I was now praying for him to meet God. (He was catholic.) His name was Timothy. I would tell him about how amazing Jesus was and that he should start asking God to show Himself to him. God was so faithful to show Himself to me when I was searching. Why wouldn't He do it for someone else? We would watch of someone named Ravi Zacharias who is an apologist and travels to universities answering questions about God. Some of the videos were really striking a chord with my friend. I continued to pray for him as we both went back to our different universities for the spring semester. My parents were scouting out some houses in the Midwest to become snowbirds. They wanted a place to retreat to for the New York winters. People usually venture to Florida, like my husband's mom, but my dad wanted to be in the mountains as he loves the outdoors. We ended up in New Mexico, and I remember the persecution being heavy again. I was crying to my best friend, Timothy, on the phone about it. It was so hard because we all shared a hotel room together the whole time. The next day, he called me to tell me that he had found Jesus! This was only a few months after our winter break. He was at a college party, and through a number of various life-changing events, God saved his life and revealed Himself to him. He then proceeded to tell me I was the one that God told him to marry! I laughed it off, telling him that he was crazy and that Jesus was my husband. I truly meant it too. Being in a place where I was so in love with my Father, I didn't want nor need any man. It wasn't on my radar at all. It was such a healthy place for a twenty-year old woman to be, and it was only through Jesus that I got there. Complete satisfaction in Him should not come in season but every day. Nothing should even come close to filling our cups like Jesus can.

A month later, Timothy flew up from Kentucky to my university in upstate New York to surprise me. We talked on the phone every day, but I still had no idea. He walked in my dorm, and I just absolutely lost it. I saw the same complete transformation in him that I had seen with my sister—a completely new person, a person full of so much life and joy. He actually only flew up for a long weekend; but throughout the course of that weekend, God had changed my heart completely about him. God revealed to me that I was supposed to marry him. God has such a sense of humor. The point where He revealed it to me was during a cardio women's workout class in the gym called Abs, Butts & Thighs. Timothy decided he wanted to do it with me and was the only man in the class. God had me turn around to look back at him, and when he was on the ground doing some funny leg stretches, He said loudly, "Jonali, this is who you are supposed to marry." Not only was I cracking up, but I was in awe because it truly came out of nowhere. I wasn't searching it out or obsessed with the idea that I needed to get married. I was completely content in Jesus. He flew back to Kentucky, and we started to date long-distance. This was so healthy at the time because we both grew in our faith, apart, for a few years. We had two different circles of solid Christian friends and had a long-distance relationship for about two years. A few months after we started dating, I remembered that list I wrote and took it out. It had been about a year since I broke up with my first boyfriend. I read the list, and in complete shock, I read a perfect description of who Timothy was. I mailed the list to Timothy. He read it and said, "This is an exact description of me.' He even asked, "How did you know all this about me?" Well, honestly, I didn't know, but God did. I believe our expectations and

His expectations are two totally different things. He never ceases to amaze us as we walk in Him.

I actually signed up to study abroad for a semester in Paris right before graduating. French was my major as I wanted to become a French teacher. Everyone in the foreign language department said you really need to immerse yourself in a country and culture in order become fluent in the language. My parents supported me in this decision, and I signed up to study at La Sorbonne in Paris, France. I remember arriving there and feeling completely overwhelmed in not understanding the language. You would think that studying French in school for almost ten years prior to going wouldn't be that challenging. Going to the basement of the girls' foyer in the first week, I called my parents, saying I wanted to go home and calling Timothy as well. They both challenged me to stick it out. That same week, a few people were handing out fliers to come to a church that happened to be a five-minute walk from the dorm I was staying in. I knew it was the Lord not only telling me to stay but bringing French Christians into my life there directly. France is mostly Catholic, so it was definitely not any ordinary thing to get invited to a nondenominational Christian church.

The second Sunday that I went, I met amazing French people my age who loved God. They invited me to come to their young adult groups. Since I was only going to be in France for about five months, I did not want to stay with the American group I came with because, if I did, I would just speak English. Paris is also a major city, so you can get by with English if you want to. My classes were obviously all in French, but I definitely needed to practice speaking. The classes were hard, and the content was difficult, and of course, all the tests and essays were in French. I trusted God with this. I started to be with my French friends on the weekends, and they invited me to their homes where I was able to experience French culture, like having homemade crepes. God opened so many amazing doors, and I didn't have to strive to find them. I brought one of the American girls to church one Sunday, and she gave her life to Jesus. She was the first person that God had used me to bring to Him. When she said yes, I was overjoyed. It was such an incredible miracle to witness. She's still following the Lord now, about fifteen years later.

One of my fondest memories of Paris was when my French friends would come over late at night, saying, "Let's go!" They had rollerblades and bikes, and they took me around major landmarks of Paris in the middle of the night, like Notre Dame and the Seine River that runs through the city. Because it was the middle of the night, there were barely any people out. It was incredible and a memory that I will never forget. There were beautiful times of intimacy as I saw the countryside of Paris and just spending time with Him. Toward the end of my time in Paris, I was able to share my testimony at a young adult group in French and not having to think about words or how to say something. It began to, finally become natural. Somehow, God helped me to get a 4.0 at one of the best universities in Paris. God did so much in the semester I had abroad there, and it all just came through relationship and trust. I'll never forget that time nor the amazing French people I met. It was definitely one of the most beautiful seasons of my life.

When I returned from France, it was summer, and I was back together with Timothy. When we were home and saw each other a bit more, we started to fight. I slowly began to (again) take my eyes off Christ and put them on Timothy. It sometimes could be so subtle and happen so fast. I was fully in love with God when I was in France but then, somehow, got distracted and started to have expectations of Timothy that became unfair. I expected him to be "prince charming" to me all the time. He turned from being a boyfriend to trying to meet my every need. The Lord started to convict me again because of the idol that he slowly became in my life. And I noticed my relationship with God to start dwindling. God asked me to break up with him because of the place he became in my life. I said to God, "What! I even wrote a list of everything I wanted in a husband, and You gave him to me!" I would argue with God as if I knew better. But I knew that I had to obey Him even though I didn't understand why. This time, obedience was a bit quicker than the last time. I was not going to wait a year to obey. I decided in my heart to let him go as it was a strong conviction. I wrote a note to him explaining that he had become an idol in my life, putting him in the place where God should be. I told him I was breaking up with him and asked him not to contact me. At the time, I was just finishing my masters as well. During this time, I was so broken but trusted in God and found myself in Him again. I fully let Him into my heart.

Only a month later, I get a text from Timothy, saying he wanted to pick me up early the next morning. It was the first time I had heard from him. In surprise, I thought, *Oh, this is interesting but okay.* He came pretty dressed up and drove me three hours to Boston, Massachusetts. We went to the aquarium. I was thinking if he was asking me to be his girlfriend. However, to my complete surprise, he proposed to me! When he got on his knee, I went into complete shock. He actually had to ask me twice because it wasn't registering. It came out of nowhere; but at the same time, it didn't. Of course I said yes, and then thanked God in the bathroom for giving him back to me.

I knew that I had let him go completely. And like Abraham, He graciously gave Timothy (or Isaac) back to me. Sometimes, God wants us to let things go to test our hearts, to see if we obey. I believe He was doing a total heart check at the time to see if I would trust Him blindly with what He was asking me to do even if it didn't make any sense. I needed that test of obedience and surrender. He even asked my parents for permission to honor them. They had requirements that I would be finished with my master's degree and that he would have a good job. We were engaged for nine months and were then married. Culturally, an Indian marrying an (White) American was unique. It was an interracial marriage but know that God is no respecter of color or nationality. He was bringing two children of God together. We planned a trip to Belize for our honeymoon, but a hurricane happened to hit at that exact time. Our travel agent needed to rebook our entire trip, and we ended up going to Aruba instead.

Chapter 4

MINISTRY AND EARLY MOTHERHOOD

Our first few years of marriage was a bit challenging. Although we both were blessed with really good full-time jobs, we had our fair share of struggles. Timothy landed a great position in a local power company and I, a French-teaching job. I also realized that I didn't just marry Timothy but his two dogs as well. Growing up, I never had dogs, so this was a huge adjustment. I was allergic too and loathed the hair everywhere, not to mention the responsibility of taking them out regularly. He had a male and a female Brittany spaniel, both not fixed. When our female was on heat, we had them in separate kennels, with doors shut, when we went to work. When home, the dogs were loose. I called the vet, asking how many percent of a chance my female was pregnant. He said 99 percent. A few months later, this newlywed couple went from two to six dogs. God started to change my heart about the dogs when they had puppies, and they turned from pets into family members. We found a great family to take a few pups. Timothy's mom took one, and we kept one. At the time, we were both in ministry as Timothy was a youth pastor at a local church. Our schedules were pretty jam-packed. But since we didn't have children yet, we were able to manage. Looking back, I wish we weren't in ministry during the first few years of marriage because

I remember arguing with him and then, minutes later, leading the youth group. It felt like hypocrisy. We also were meeting with the pastor and his wife, talking about our challenges, and they definitely helped us. We then shifted to being leaders in a young adult ministry while Timothy was working and doing his master's degree.

At a leadership conference, I heard the audible voice of God for the first time. He told me to pioneer a Christian group at a large secular campus. I chuckled at God because here I was, still a bit young at age twenty-six, and He wanted a quiet Indian girl to start something when I had no idea of how to start it. The leadership conference talked about leaders not necessarily being the most qualified and pointed out examples like David in the Bible. There is a quote: "God doesn't call the qualified, He qualifies the called." It was funny because before God called me, I told Timothy on the way to the conference that it was crazy that I was attending this conference because I never saw myself as a leader. Sometimes, however, that is the best place to be when God calls you to do something, when you're not striving to seek it out, but rather God just speaks and opens up doors on your behalf. This is what He did for the college group. Satan spoke whispers to me my whole life, saying I would amount to nothing, that God wouldn't have a plan for me, and that I would just be a quiet, shy, Indian girl the rest of my life. So there was much doubt when He called me because it seemed like a daunting task, especially for someone like me who wasn't equipped. I had to obey though, so I began to take small steps to see what God would do.

Firstly, out of nowhere, he brought me to a couple of Christian students who attended this university. I told them of what God had spoken to me and asked them if they wanted to help. They were completely on board and said they would do whatever it took to get this group going. I wouldn't have been able to do this without students, and God dropped them on my lap. He then brought a pastor on board who would help support it. Our meetings started small but in the second year grew. The group finally got SA (student association) recognition so it could start renting out rooms and get financial help to run it. We had evangelistic outreaches where we had creative ideas—for example, beta pong (where you'd have to throw a ball and get it in a fish bowl to win a fish). Students would get free pizza at meetings where we would share the gospel. Once the group grew, we were able to have student leaders organize going door-to-door, praying for people, or praying for people in the middle of the night. One of the most amazing miracles we had witnessed was Timothy praying over someone completely intoxicated then seeing that person a few minutes later sober and able to walk completely normal. He later gave his life to Christ and had a Christian background. But after God touched his life, it was easy for him to say yes!

After pioneering the group and getting it running for a few years, we had the peace to move on. We actually put our house on the market to move closer to the campus. But after already moving into our mom's house for a transition period, God was clear that it was time to give it up. I fell pregnant with my second shortly after. The original plan of living with mother-in-law for six months ended up getting longer as we decided to just stay and have the baby there. I gave birth to my daughter, and she screamed for the first three months. My son was colic as well, so unfortunately, I had two infants who screamed nonstop for the first three months of their lives.

With Elijah, I had to bounce him on one of those exercise balls to get him to calm down. And for Priya, she just needed to be held all the time. I was not getting any sleep, probably only two to three hours of broken sleep a night. I went through a lot of postpartum depression because of this and just felt completely depleted all the time. I had difficulty nursing and producing enough milk for them because of the stress and lack of rest. Thankfully, after three months hit, the constant screaming stopped, and they both started sleeping better at night with longer stretches. I finally was feeling somewhat normal again. When Priya was about three months old and the colic was better, a stomach bug went through our house. After about forty-eight hours, everyone got better except me. I didn't understand why as my body usually just bounced back to normal, but it could have been because I hadn't had gotten proper sleep for three months, and I was really stressed out. The nausea persisted, then the dizziness started, then the back pain, vision blurriness, sensitivity to loud noises, chills in my brain, a weakened immune system, a new sensitivity to certain foods, crazy torment in my mind, mind fog, the loss of weight, and too many more symptoms to name. I was a full-time mom at this point with a baby and toddler, not living in my own home, and my husband was away roughly ten hours a day. I pleaded with God after seeing doctors and getting a huge amount of blood tests that had no answers. "I need answers!" I screamed to Him, and He gently replied, "I am the answer." I quickly replied, "No, Lord, I want answers so I can take medicine and be done with this!" That was the end of the conversation as He didn't respond to my controlling response. I didn't know what He really meant at the time. But after a while, it became clear.

CHAPTER 5

MY WILDERNESS
(OR JOB) SEASON

A part of me was angry at God, another part of me was hurt, and yet another part of me was just completely confused. I had been healthy my entire life, never had to go to the hospital for anything besides giving birth, and now, all of a sudden, every part of my body was completely being attacked, and my mind was following my body in thinking this was the end for me. How is that even possible? Does God heal all the time? No, not based on my experience. Why was He being silent with what was wrong with me? What did He mean, "I am the answer?" Answer to what? Functioning became less and less easy. I had a baby and a toddler that needed 100 percent of my attention. I also had two dogs to take care of. I had to pray to take a shower, drive, make food for my toddler, and many other things I normally did with no problem. How, now, was I going to be able to take care of the kids in the hardest stage of motherhood physically? I came to an end of myself and cried all the time. I was turning to God only when I needed Him. Then the Holy Spirit gently spoke to me and asked how long it had been since I was fully surrendered to God. What? What does that have to do with the current situation I was in? Was I in control or allowing Him to be in control? In the last few years of my life, especially after having children, I realized how much the spirit of control had taken over me. I started to realize how far I was from God. I didn't even know how much I had let stress (which was my own fault) affect me. I was ruled by worst case scenarios, fear, anxiety, and depression. Slowly I went from having a relationship with God to just going through the motions. It certainly was not overnight, but it was a slow progression. I had stopped realizing how important it was to get in the Word, pray, and just spend time with Him. I had fallen away from my first love and into the world and only just became aware of it.

When I became aware of these deeper things, Timothy called me from work, telling me he thought I have Lyme disease based upon talking to some of his coworkers. My first reaction was one of surprise because, although that disease was so prevalent where I lived, I had never found a tick on me. He said his coworkers have had similar symptoms, and I should get a blood test for it. My second reaction was of relief, still thinking I could take meds for this, and it would be gone.

I went to see the best Lyme specialist there was in the northeast area and drove a couple hours for my first appointment. The doctor straightaway clinically diagnosed me based upon my symptoms. He said all of my symptoms were evidence that I had Lyme. I began antibiotics right away as my blood test was sent in to a lab in California. The results came back 50 percent positive. A part of me was relieved, but a part of me was still upset because it was not definitive. Fifty percent? Really? I was desperate for answers, but now it was only half a chance that I had it. Doctors say that with this disease, the Lyme bacteria can hide and reappear, and the tests are never 100 percent accurate. Doctors and people also say that you can have Lyme the rest of your life, especially if you don't catch it right away, because of the bacteria's ability to spread throughout your whole nervous system and go to places where antibiotics can't reach. This is the worst disease you can have if you struggle with fear.

Again, I was thinking to myself, I might have this awful disease, but I might not. I may have it the rest of my life; I may not. My mind was going crazy. For almost two months of taking heavy antibiotics, doxycycline, day and night, I wondered, *Were they helping?*

It appeared like they were sometimes, but other times it seemed like they did not. The side effects definitely seemed harsh on my body as well. One of the side effects was having nightmares. I don't remember having many nightmares, but the medication was messing with my mind. It seemed like I was going absolutely insane. Sometimes it was hard to tell what was the medication and what was the sickness. I wasn't getting better. I got to a point where I had to move into my mom's house to have more help with the kids. I thought, *If we just moved there for a month, I could sleep and rest, and my body would surely get better.* I needed to be in control. I was trying to find alternatives in the natural realm instead of going to God. I began to get so bad physically that I had visions of people coming to my parents' house to say goodbye to me. I had pictures of my funeral and what people would say about me. I felt completely trapped.

I told Timothy to find a good Christian wife to take care of our children because in my mind at the time, my life was about to be over. A part of me wanted to give up after trying medications and feeling absolutely powerless from being completely sick. It felt like I was drowning in a deep ocean with waves constantly going over my head and no strength to keep continuing to breathe for air. My body seemed like it was just rapidly losing all the strength it once had and every part was not functioning properly anymore. At the same time, the voice speaking to me was only speaking about death and giving up, that life was over for me. The spirit of death was hovering over me constantly, and the more I entertained these thoughts, the worse I got physically.

After living with my parents for a month, and that month of complete rest didn't help, I moved back to my mother-in-law's home. Timothy was absolutely amazing, not only taking over when he got home from work but, more importantly, reading the Word to me, constantly encouraging me. I needed a voice of truth over the continual lies going on in my mind. With Timothy speaking life over the situation, hope started to come back in small glimpses. Sometimes Timothy would just sternly look at me in the eye, and say, "Jonali, don't say that," or "Don't think that." It was like God was using him to battle the torment going on in my mind. Had I not had a solid

Christian husband who believed in healing, I probably would not have made it as he played an enormous role in my getting better. For me, it was a huge help that he prayed for the sick and believed in healing. At this point in our marriage, we had walked through persecution, miscarriage, seeing God save both of our children when they were infants, and various other trials. We had seen victory but also experienced defeat. It had been about six months since I first became sick and now had a pretty huge revelation.

Chapter 6

RENEWING OF THE MIND

I never realized the depravity of my thought life until I got sick. Entertaining worst-case scenarios was normal to me. Worry, fear, depression, and anxiety had a grip on me that I thought was normal. Being in control of my life seemed normal, but it was far from it. Never really having a steadfast peace seemed common. When I got sick, all these things came right to the surface as they would come and go. Having children seemed to exasperate everything. The early stages of motherhood were hard, and the fact that I was relying on my own strength made everything worse. I was completely stuck, wishing I could just wake up, and the nightmare was over. I treated God like a genie in a bottle. Shouting scriptures on healing but not really believing them as Satan's voice was louder in my mind. It seemed like I was a Pharisee, knowing all the right things to say, but my heart was far from Him. I had enough head knowledge to tell me what to do during this season according to the word of God.

I wanted the healing, but I didn't want the Healer. I wanted to take medicine but miss out on the process. I wanted my physical body to be well but ignore the depravity of the state of my mind. I wanted a quick fix but didn't want to go through a time of repenting for the years I had missed in the power of obedience and surrender, especially in the area of my mind. I was blind to all of this before I was sick. My heart hardened over time, and I wasn't even aware of it.

On the surface, everything looked good, but I was spiritually dying on the inside. When well-known Christians fall away, it used to surprise me, but it no longer does. It is so easy to put on a front in front of people, but it is a whole different ball game to live completely transparent in front of people with humility that you've "missed the mark." I am so thankful that I wasn't in any ministry at the time but only serving the local church. It was an extremely humbling time, especially after leading a college ministry that was very successful.

I had two choices: I could keep going from doctor to doctor, continue to get more blood tests for more solid answers, keep taking antibiotics (that I was not even sure were working), or I could actually turn from my sin, repent, and reenter my relationship with God that had become cold. Again, I was having this revelation now about six months into the sickness. I've tried "route A" for six months, and nothing was really changing. I decided to finally repent and turn from the sin that had turned me into nothing but a life of dead branches that were withering away slowly.

I had had enough and was in a desperate fight for my life, knowing that God was the Author of life. I needed to take a journey from my head knowledge of God back to my heart. Fear was one of the largest strongholds. Knowing that "perfect love cast out all fear, because fear has to do with punishment" (1 John 4:18), God spoke to me gently and said, "I want to take you through a season of getting a revelation of My love for you, Jonali." I knew that I could not work off fear but that He had to take the opposite spirit of fear and take me through a journey of being enveloped by His love.

When I first accepted Christ into my heart, I never went through a journey of allowing Him to love me until I was complete in it. I think that was why I fell away when I went to college because I was still trying to fill a void that only He could. I didn't get it right in believing the simple truth that He loved me no matter what, and He loved me with a deep agape love more than any earthly man could even come close to. He spoke with such a gentle spirit, saying that all I needed to do was receive His love, nothing else. He told me not to strive in my relationship with Him but just to meditate on how much He loves me and take to just a couple scriptures to soak my heart. It seemed like I was a desert, and it hadn't rained for close to a decade.

As I meditated on how much He loved me and actually received His love, God started to let the rain moisten the dryness in my heart. My spirit began to fill with joy and hope again as I began to believe the simple truth of my Father loving me so much that He sent down His only Son to die for me. We quote this as Christians all the time, but if we actually believe it, this truth should never grow old and should overwhelm us every day. I had to do absolutely nothing to earn or deserve it. I started to realize how depraved I was because I didn't receive His unconditional love for me. As a parent, I was able to soak this concept in a little deeper. The fear, anxiety, racing of my heart, entertaining of worst-case scenarios began to slowly disappear as the foundation of love was being built in my soul. Hope started to birth again in my life. Love began to be my forefront. The spirit of death that was hovering over me started to disappear. I noticed the patience increased with my children. I began to apologize to my husband for the way I had treated him during the past decade of marriage and having more of a loving heart toward my family. He was doing such a deep surgery in my heart that was so needed. I was completely vulnerable, allowing Him to work in areas I had never given Him before. I didn't work for this; it was who God had already made me to be. I just wasn't living in the identity that He created me to be. My hardened heart began to melt as I became vulnerable to His love and mercy toward me. My life began to transform. I had stopped asking God to heal me as that wasn't my focus anymore. I wasn't allowing the symptoms to rock me because His love was transforming me. This overwhelmed me. Nothing else seemed to matter. I was falling in love again, and nothing could touch that. I found a strength in mothering my children through the illness and having joy, no matter what my current situation and circumstance was.

I've learned, over the years, the importance of obedience and surrender especially in the area of renewing my mind. God spoke to me and said that those two areas are His love languages. We all have heard that we each have different love languages. For example, mine are words of affirmation and touch. If my husband were to speak negatively over me or abuse me, it was probably the worst thing he could do. I receive love the best through him speaking words of love over me or rubbing my back. I believe it is the same way with God. The opposite of obedience is disobedience, and the opposite of surrender is control. Sometimes we have to have seasons in our lives and ask God, "Lord, will You please highlight some areas of my life where I am not surrendered to You?" or, "Lord, show me some areas where I am not obeying You." Sometimes it's not a pretty picture. God, however, loves those He disciplines. I think parents can understand this concept well. "My son, do not make light of the Lord's discipline, and do not lose heart when He rebukes you because the Lord disciplines the one that he loves, and He chastens everyone he accepts as His son." Endure hardship as discipline; God is treating you as His children. For what children are not disciplined by their father? If you are not disciplined, and everyone undergoes discipline, then you are not legitimate, not true sons and daughters at all. Moreover, we have all had human fathers who disciplined us, and we respect them for it. How much more should we submit to the Father of spirits and live! They disciplined us for a little while as they thought best; but God disciplines us for our good in order that we may share in his holiness. No discipline seems pleasant at the time but painful. Later on, however, it produces a harvest of righteousness and peace for those who have been trained by it. Hebrews 12:5–11.

I hadn't realized the rebellion in my heart from years of unrepented sin especially in these two areas. Pride and lack of trust led me down a path of disillusionment and fear. I became so numb to the thoughts that tormented me for years. I didn't realize how paralyzed I was to these dark thoughts going through my mind all day long. I never realized how many lies I had believed in for years and how normal they were to me. Although I was a Christian and knew the word, I never went through the process of what 2 Corinthians 5 said to do: "To demolish arguments and every pretension that sets itself up against the knowledge of God, and to take every thought captive and make it obedient to Christ." In the *Cambridge Dictionary*, a pretension is "the appearance of being more important or more serious than there is reason for." It's an illusion or something that seems true, but it's not. God instructs us to take every thought captive, which means we take a hold of it, capture it like making it a prisoner, and then making obedient to God. So if it is a lie, we speak the Word—truth—against it. I remember I was in the middle of worshipping God, after I broke up with Timothy, and sensed His presence all around me. I heard this voice say, "You are going to die young." Immediately, my heart was full of fear. For an entire year, I was paralyzed, thinking I was going to die, as I thought this was what the Lord said to me. I did not know at the time that the devil comes to kill, steal, and destroy, but God comes to give life and give it abundantly (John 10:10). This fear came with me as a newlywed. Timothy would tell me it wasn't God, but for some reason, it was hard for me to believe it since I heard the voice in the midst of worshipping God. I was so blind at the time, and because I had been a puppet to Satan for so long, his voice was normal to me.

I felt overwhelmed, as I started to realize how many lies I had believed during the time I had been born again. My knowledge of the Bible was good enough to start somewhere. The Lord showed me a picture of my brain and, basically, how there was a garden in my mind that had never been weeded. The fruit, vegetable, and flowers were all overgrown in the garden where it looked like it hadn't been tended for years, like someone abandoned their home and just left it completely. It wasn't something I could tame with weed killer.

The Lord said it was time to weed to pull the roots out. There were decades of lies in there and wanting for God to snap His finger to have a renewed mind overnight. Although I believe God is the worker of miracles, I believe, for this, it was going to take some work on my part. In a state of being overwhelmed, crying out to the Lord, imploring, "Lord, where do I even begin?" I had years of unrepentance, being in control, anxiety, fear, and much more. Jesus gently said, "Jonali, just receive my love." It was His tender mercy that blew my overwhelmed state of mind to just focus on His love for me. He said not to worry about all the other lies but to only meditate on scriptures of His love for me. He said to "listen to His voice" and understand that His voice sounds like life and life abundant, not to steal, kill, and destroy as it states the difference in John 10:10 about

Jesus and the devil. I laid down the stress from being overwhelmed and took God at the word He spoke to me, which was only one thing: His love.

As I started to take hold of how much the Creator of the universe loved me, I became completely overwhelmed by this truth alone. I never spent time doing this when I first received Him into my life. I didn't know how much time it was going to take to get a revelation of this, but I trusted Him to not move from His love. I would spend hours, days, and weeks letting the love of God soak in and start to be full of joy. It was simple, my Father in heaven loved me without condition. He loved me simply because I was His daughter. One simple truth: The Creator of the universe is in love with me so much so that He sent His only Son to die for me so that I could be free. This is absolutely profound. I heard once that you can't build a house without a foundation. Logically, this makes sense. How can I move forward as a Christian if I don't know that I know that I know that He loves me? After a decade of being a Christian, I hadn't let the very foundation of my faith take root of how much He loved me. I was doing all the right things, going to church, meeting with a mentor, reading the word but clearly didn't have a grasp on His love because fear had ruled my life. I still believed the lie that I had to behave a certain way for Him to love me. This is also what Hinduism taught me; you are loved if you behave properly. If you don't, bad things would happen in the next life. They call that karma. We hear it all the time. God loves you. But how many times do we take those words, and they go through one ear and out the other?—too many to count. What if we meditated on that over and over again, that we are fully loved and accepted? All believers need such a revelation on the simplicity of the gospel. I believe we all need to go through a time of simply receiving His love especially when we live in a fear-driven world. I had to believe the fact that He loved me even though I was going through the absolute worst trial of my life. He never promised we would be without trials just because we are believers.

Chapter 7

PERFECT LOVE CASTS OUT FEAR

The constant nausea, back pain, fatigue, vision blurriness, light sensitivity, weakness, sound sensitivity, and dizziness I held on to this truth about love and it became my forefront. Somehow, His love became louder than the symptoms in my body. It was as if something in my spirit quieted my flesh. I reached the point where I wasn't focused on getting healed anymore because I was too wrapped up with His love for me. The love started to be so overwhelming that I could focus on Him more than my symptoms. Colossians 3:1–3 says, "Since you have then been raised with Christ, set your hearts on things above, where Christ is, seated at the right hand of God. Set your mind on things above, not on earthly things. For you died, and your life is hidden with Christ in God." So it says, first, set your heart on things above, and then it reiterates the same point, saying, set your mind on things above. I don't think that we can afford to glance over instructions like this. God wants our hearts and minds on Him. At the time, it was easy for me to focus on my symptoms because they, literally, were causing me to not be able to function. I saw, however, the shift in my spirit take place when I was overwhelmed with His love to the point where the symptoms wouldn't even phase me. It was a complete miracle.

Everything in my body, from head to toe, was not functioning properly, yet my mind was being renewed minute by minute, hour by hour, day by day. The symptoms weren't as loud as His love and seemed as if they weren't even there, as if they were. Some people say, "Mind over matter." Maybe it's like heaven over earth. It was as if I was on a honeymoon with God, and yet everything was trying to shout at me, whether it was physical symptoms, doctor's words saying I would be sick forever, or (Christian) friends telling me their horror stories of Lyme. I could list so many more strategic ploys of the enemy, trying to get me off focus and fall into fear (a familiar spirit). But I was falling in love with Jesus over and over again. Jesus was literally melting away the fear with His love every time I wouldn't listen or bow down to it. Every time a symptom would come, I would say, "Thank You, Lord, that You love me and that You gave your Son for me." Medical advice would come and to try and instill fear or my being sick forever or even dying. Instead, I would speak, "Thank You, Jesus, that it is Your desire to heal me as it was already done at the cross. I thank You that I will not die but live and proclaim what You have done" (Psalm 118:17). I had to proclaim the truth over the lie even though the lies seemed or appeared to be my reality. I needed to come to a place of believing the unseen until it started to become my reality. I began to understand what living by the Spirit was actually like and not living by carnality.

The Lord spoke loudly to me, saying, "I want you to be able to see more with your eyes closed than with your eyes open," meaning to live in places where I set my mind on things above so not to be swayed by my senses, whereby the place in heavenly realms speaks louder than my sight, smell, taste, touch, and sound. He taught me how to worship again. And to be clear, I am not talking about lip service. I am talking about true, genuine worship where it is not singing songs to God. I have so many memories at a local playground, pushing my daughter on the swing while my son was content playing the sandbox. I was worshipping God, saying out loud how much I loved Him. I didn't care what people thought if they heard me as my audience was God, not man.

Realizing I wasn't in a "woe is me" state of life anymore, I moved from drowning to staying afloat. The Lord was to show me the how-to. I began to be able to function again and not have to pray for the little things I once did, like take a shower or have the strength to put my children down at night. I started to regain strength and see life with a bit more of a clear lens. He was "weeding my garden" with one profound truth—that He loved me unconditionally. Once this was becoming my foundation, it was easy to throw away all the lies (or weeds) that I had once allowed to grow. It wasn't overwhelming anymore. The only truth that I was overwhelmed by was His simple love for me. I realized that I had believed so many lies over time that created and fed the constant stress, fear, and anxiety I had over myself. Things, like depression, were a bit selfish because I was always thinking about me, woe was me, and why this was happening to me. There was a lot of self-pity. If the God of the universe sent His only Son to die for me, then how in the world could I even be depressed? There can be no room for that because not only does He loves me, but there is so much more of an inheritance I have as a believer. At that point, I was only scratching the surface!

Chapter 8

THE PRACTICAL AND LEANING ON THE BODY OF CHRIST

I listened to sermons on renewing the mind and on healing; those were the topics that I was after at the time. In my mind, based on circumstance I had at the time, I believed it was God's will to heal only sometimes; but in the Bible, I saw that Jesus healed every person that came to Him. There are too many scriptures that support healing. Also, when you are fighting for your life, you can't be wishy-washy, as I didn't want to be how James 1: 6–8 talked about: "But when you ask, you must believe and not doubt, because the one who doubts is like a wave of the sea, blown and tossed by the wind. That person should not expect to receive anything from the Lord. Such a person is double-minded and unstable in all they do." I had to have a militant-like faith and stand on the word no matter what I was feeling or on symptoms I was currently having. I understand my experience has been, "Sally gets healed, and Billy doesn't," but the word of God (truth) surpasses my earthly experience, and I don't have answers as to why some get healed and some do not.

Did I wrestle with that question for years in my Christian life? Of course. However, when you are fighting for your life, you don't really have that option to battle that question and go back and forth. You have to decide what you believe and stick with it. So for me, I could either go by my experience or what the Bible says. I was reading healing books by Kenneth Hagin and Derek Prince because they are very black-and-white people, and so am I. I needed a black-and-white theology, not a gray one. I had to have clear vision and an unwavering mind—a helmet of salvation. Just because you give your life to Jesus doesn't mean you don't have to regularly wear your armor. We need to be cognizant of the enemy's schemes. As believers, we are a target. And if we let the enemy attack us constantly and don't put on our armor, we will eventually give up the fight and cave into the circumstance. He has given us the keys to overcome, and everyone's journey looks different; but our swords remain the same. The word of God is absolute truth, and we need to come to a transition period from the head to the heart. We must know Jesus, not know about Him. This is the difference between relationship and religion. My son, Elijah, knows his father. He lives with him, eats meals with him, learns from him, plays with him, and spends time with him. Another child doesn't know his father like Elijah does but knows about him. There is a huge difference, yet a lot of Christians still struggle today with religion versus relationship. Again, Jesus healed every single person He laid hands on. He is my example, not man.

At the time, I was in contact with a mentor who told me about a website that has daily prophetic words. At the time, I didn't know much about prophecy or the prophetic, all I knew was that it was one of the gifts listed in 1 Corinthians 12. God started to introduce me to it through this website. I learned that prophetic words can be encouraging, edifying, or a warning. I knew the Holy Spirit was prompting me to read the site regularly. I started reading words from one author named Lana Vawser from Australia. It was as if she was in my living room, watching my life. She wasn't just reading my mail; she had a download of my hard drive. Every word she said had so much accuracy that God used her to really speak to me for about a year. "Pleasant words are like a honeycomb, sweetness to the soul and health to the bones" (Proverbs 16:24). These pleasant, prophetic words helped to bring health to my body because of the hope to my spirit. It also sparked an interest of the gift of prophecy to me. Going back to Hinduism, it isn't really known as a religion that speaks many positive things. In fact, it has a reputation for being negative. It is full of worst-case scenarios and fear-driven words. The glass is always half empty. I was so drawn to the prophetic because it is speaking life and not death. There is not only a thick spirit of fear attached to the religion I was brought up in but also a spirit of death. No wonder I craved words of life so much! Lana's words were refreshing and from the Lord. I will never cease to thank the Lord for her obedience. She is a friend now as God brought us together in the Sunshine Coast of Australia for a season. This is a whole other story!

As my intimacy began with the Lord once again, it was easier to focus on Him than what was going on around me. We didn't have our own home. And because of different circumstances, like having a second child and becoming ill, we weren't able to get one. We had put offers on a few houses, but they didn't go through. I didn't understand what was going on at the time. It seemed like everything was against me—all the natural circumstances, sickness, not having our own home, the cares of watching after a baby and toddler while my husband was gone at least ten hours a day. If my eyes were only on me, the stress of everything would have overwhelmed me. If my eyes were on Jesus and my focus on how much He loved me, in letting go, and believing His promises, I overcame in God. But He gave me the ability to choose. It was as if I was Peter, and Jesus told me to walk on the water. When my eyes were fixed on Him, I could do it; but when they were on the wind or waves, I sank.

About a year into the sickness, my husband and I decided to go to a conference with some powerful speakers a few hours away. A woman, who I had admired for years, was the keynote speaker. Her name was Heidi Baker. She has gone through many serious, life-threatening trials. God spoke to her about being a missionary to Mozambique, Africa. The first few years were hard and consisted of rescuing babies out of a dumpster. After the ministry had been going for a few years, her life became in danger of being stoned at, numerous death threats, sickness with malaria where her life was in danger, her husband having cerebral malaria, and numerous other attacks. With God, she had overcome every one of those circumstances. This is why she is one of my heroines in the faith. Through adversity, she relied on Jesus for each and every battle and has come out strong.

I attended a breakfast seminar she was having where she was taking three questions. With easily over one hundred people in the room, I pleaded with God that she would take my question. With little time left and only one question left, she (amazingly) picked me! It is rare that you are able to have a chat with these speakers at huge conferences, but God ordained it because He used her to speak to me. Of course, with everything I was going through, I asked her, "How did you manage to keep your head up when you were fighting for your life?" Before I could finish my question, I broke down in tears. The first thing she did was hug me. She showed me His love. Her heart was full of so much life and love; it was incredible. If she didn't say a word more, that would have been enough. But she had a word of knowledge and confirmed three things that the Lord had been already speaking, which were, "Fix your eyes on Jesus," "believe what He said is true," "He rewires your brain." Those words cut directly into my heart. She then had everyone pray for me. It was one of the most beautiful moments in my life. It felt as though that it was the hand and heart of God in the exact timing when I needed it. God is so good at dropping love and His loud voice through others at the time we need it. Heidi wasn't only the breath of fresh love when I needed it but confirmation to everything He was saying. When someone speaks so poignantly to you, when they don't know you, or what is going on in your life, it is it extremely special and comforting especially when you are fighting for your life. You are desperate for life and trying to move in rhythms of everyday life. God will give you rhythms to move in, and He will give you what you need when you need it, as His grace is sufficient in our weakest moments.

Something really great to do is to find a couple people who you admire, look up to, and also have a solid biblical foundation. Some of my women heroes are Joyce Meyer and Christine Caine. They have both been through things, like rape and, through Christ, have found healing and now empower other women (and men) to walk in victory, not as victims. They are older than me, and I know that Joyce Meyer is, actually, Christine Caine's mentor. They both have had health scares, like cancer, and have come through victoriously. They are the type of women who, if a circumstance comes along, don't quiver in fear but, already having on their armor, are ready for the battle. Whether seeing them live or listening to them on the radio, they have truly encouraged me in a lot of different ways! They not only are international speakers, but both have nonprofit organizations as well. I completely recommend both of them and their books to you. Usually when I am encouraged by a few different people, I check their speaking schedules to see if I can make it to one of their conferences or talks. It never hurts to do what you can to fit something like this into your schedule if you are able!

I was recently able to go the women's conference at Hillsong called Colour in Sydney, Australia, where Christine Caine was the keynote speaker. I asked a few women in my life to support me in going, and they did. So Timothy watched the children for a long weekend, and I flew there. The weekend was nothing short of powerful, energizing, and refreshing! As much as I never want to be a conference "junkie," I am sensitive to which conferences to invest money and time into. Most people can agree that conferences can give you a great high, but then after it's over, it is back to usual, and nothing has changed. I think we need to understand, as believers, that conferences are meant to encourage and take us deeper into God and never be a substitute. They are meant to add, not replace. We should never find ourselves dependent on them, otherwise we will go from conference to conference with a short-term high but a long-term emptiness. We are meant to have a relationship with God and allow Him, and Him alone, to fill those empty placed that only He can fill. Anything on top of that is icing on the cake! This can go not only for conferences but church, friendships, spouses, small groups, etc.

Chapter 9

Transformation

As time went on, God was renewing my mind every day. It seemed as if I was actually transforming. He started to speak to me through the metamorphosis that happens when a caterpillar changes into a butterfly. He taught me that Christians can invite Him into their lives solely to just get into heaven. But if they aren't surrendering their life to Him daily, they are in danger of never moving past the caterpillar stage. They can go through all the motions, like go to church, read their Bible, and even be in full-time ministry; but inwardly, there is no transformation. That is how it was with me for years of my walk with God, but God showed me that there is no transformation if we don't renew our minds. Biblically, according to Romans 12:2, this is a true statement. We could even get to the pupa stage and never get past it. For caterpillars, when they are in the pupa or cocoon stage, it looks like the caterpillar could be just resting; but on the inside, it is rapidly changing. When the caterpillar has transformed and changed inside the pupa, it will emerge from the chrysalis. At first, its wings are soft and folded against the body because it now has new parts. It will rest for a few days when it's outside of the chrysalis, and it will pump blood into the wings to get them to flap then eventually fly. In the final stages, the adult butterflies are constantly looking to reproduce, then the cycle will start all over. The Lord also spoke to me that some get to the stage where they form into a butterfly but are never able to spread their wings. They stay inside the pupa and are too afraid to spread their wings, thus preventing them from sharing the gospel to others, and then others never get the chance of being introduced to God. There are fewer Christians who are flying than who are staying in the pupa. It could be past wounds that were never healed or caught up with things of the world or life circumstances that are too heavy for a human being to carry. I've been in many seasons of my life where fear, circumstance, pain, or just complacency crippled me from having a relationship with God. Those were the times in my life where I felt most empty. I looked for longing and satisfaction in other things, friendships, my husband, food, coffee, chocolate, work, etc.

A mirror can be symbolic of so many things. Personally, I usually like to avoid the mirror because I don't always love what I see. In the midst of my sickness, I looked fairly skinny. I would eat but not know where the food was going. I remember saying I couldn't wait to look normal again because every time I looked in the mirror, it was just a reminder of how sick I was. So now that I realized the Bible completely supports that Jesus heals, and it was part of His sacrifice on the cross for me, I decided I would start to speak the truth of God's word in front of the mirror so that I was speaking life over my body. To be completely honest, at the beginning, it felt like lip service. I was speaking it but not wholly believing it with my heart. I didn't feel anything. I just knew God wanted me to do it. After doing this for a few weeks, something started to really shift in my spirit man. I began to realize that it was the enemy causing the infliction, which caused a righteous anger within me. I realized that I didn't have to live with this for the rest of my life. Doctors, friends, and people around me would tell me that their uncle or their friend had Lyme disease and that it became worse and worse. Some people tell me their horror stories of people having to be in a wheelchair or not live life normally anymore.

They say if you don't catch Lyme right away, the bacteria from the tick can get into your bloodstream and start to spread throughout your body. It can debilitate you. There was even a time where Elijah's knee blew up, and the doctor diagnosed it with Lyme, so he actually went on antibiotics too for a couple weeks. The thought of having it when Priya was in my womb caused me to think she could have it as well. So here I was as a mother with a baby and toddler, now feeling guilty, believing I missed a tick in my toddler's skin and maybe passing it along to my daughter while pregnant. Between the horror stories and my kids possibly having Lyme, I had to make another black-and-white choice. Was I going to listen to these horror stories and believe them for me, or was I going to take God's word and believe it as truth? Was I going to entertain the possibility of my children having it and fall into fear, or would I also believe the promises of God over my children? I am a firm believer that if you entertain or give thought to something like these situations, you empower it. So even if it's not true, and it is a lie, it has the power to turn into something real if I think about it constantly and feed those fears.

So back to the mirror! Because I was speaking the truth out loud and because the healing scriptures were fresh in my memory, it helped me. So because of this, it helped me to not believe worst-case scenarios and other people's horror stories. It helped me to actually guard my mind. Because there is another scripture that says, "Life and death is in the power of the tongue" (Proverbs 18:21), so I believe that speaking it out not only had power to my body but to my mind as well. God was renewing my mind and my thoughts. I didn't have the strength to do it; but when I surrendered it to the Lord and gave up the control, He had the ability to be strong in my weakness. I remember my friend came over, and she had a picture of me. It was me as a superhero. Superheroes have different gifts. Some can disappear; some can have a lot of strength; some can fly. She said the Lord focused on my mind. I had this amazing helmet that really stood out, and it showed my mind was actually my superpower because God was making the weakness strong. From the time I was a child to early thirties, my mind had been a complete devil's playground.

Back to the picture of being in the garden that had never been weeded, completely overgrown with weeds that were taking over any life that had tried to grow, the roots of all the plants or flowers didn't have any room to grow because the weeds would take all the water. I realized I couldn't weed an overgrown, thirty-year-old garden. That seemed like a lost cause. Why tend to it when it looked absolutely hopeless? If someone were to see the overgrown garden full of weeds, I assure you, they would never take the time to weed it. God said, "Jonali, one weed at a time." This translated to one lie at a time. Take one thought captive every time. It seemed like a completely overwhelming, daunting task. He gave me hope and told me He would do the work; all I had to do was to obey in the area of my mind. If I knew something was a lie, all I had to do was believe the truth over the lie. In the beginning, it was hard work. But freedom was just around the corner. I was just being obedient to what the Lord asked me to do. Becoming a marine isn't an overnight thing; it takes time, dedication, and strength. It seemed like I had no chance, that it was completely impossible. But He promised me that "with Him, all things are possible," and "His strength is perfect in weakness." Although sometimes, it was so hard to believe the word over my symptoms, He asked me to trust Him. My body was speaking a lot louder than the word, especially in the beginning. It seemed as if nothing was happening, and I was wasting time. He asked me to keep going, to persevere. We also glory in our sufferings because we know that suffering produces perseverance; perseverance, character; and character, hope (Romans 5:4).

God's love language is obedience. It's like when you are a parent and your child simply obeys, isn't that the best feeling in the world? How much more is it like that with God? I could not see the end, but I knew it was going to be a long road ahead. But that is the place of faith that God loves to move in, when we can't see anything changing or shifting, but we are still believing. Sometimes the battle can take days, weeks, months, or even years. God doesn't see time like we do. He sees your heart and cares about that the most! It seemed, when I took one step forward, Satan came and brought me two steps back. He doesn't play fair, and we are in a battle. We need to recognize Who we carry. God had a garden full of flowers and plants that were just waiting to grow, and the water it needed was my obedience!

Don't we all love the story of David and Goliath? The shepherd boy or complete underdog conquering the Philistine giant! We love to teach this to our children and reenact this scene for a church play.

But what about all the time leading up to the battle? David didn't have a "name" growing up, but he was faithful in the little things. But David said to Saul, "Your servant was tending to his father's sheep. When a lion or a bear came and took a lamb from the flock, I went after him and attacked him, and rescued it from his mouth; and when he rose up against me, I seized him by his beard and struck him and killed him. Your servant has killed both the lion and the bear" (1 Samuel 17:34–36). David didn't just conquer Goliath all of a sudden. He was in training.

There was a time once where I threw recyclables in the normal garbage, and the Holy Spirit was saying to me, "Jonali, go back to the garbage and put what goes in the recycling into the recyclable garbage." Is it sin to throw away recyclable garbage into the normal garbage? No. But we are to steward the earth well and obey the laws of the land. Ever since, I have always organized my garbage accordingly. God is constantly speaking, whether it is as a still, small voice as His or as loud as a trumpet, the question remains; Are we listening? Are there times where I still disobey? Absolutely. However, it becomes dangerous if we disobey over and over and over again because that is the path that leads to destruction. More dangerous is our conscience being seared—meaning, our ability to discern right and wrong will diminish. If we ignore Him repeatedly, our conviction and His still, small voice will lessen, and He will just give up and give us over to our sin. We never want to get to that place. I have too many times to the point where I have questioned if I was a true believer or not. After giving my life to Jesus more than eighteen years ago, I cannot afford to waste any more time. Life is too precious and short. There are too many people hurting and need God. And if we hold the keys to life, to a dark and dying world, we cannot be selfish. Eternity is too important. There is no room for that in Jesus. He asked us to give Him our lives, not a part of our life.

Chapter 10

A Major Life Change

There is no room for being lukewarm in Jesus. I have found myself in too many seasons of complacency or being apathetic. The problem is, Jesus addressed this specifically to the church in Laodicea in Revelation 3. In verses 5–21, He addressed neither being hot or cold. He went on to say He would spit you out of His mouth. The Laodiceans understood this "lukewarm" analogy because their water came from an aqueduct from a spring miles away, and it came lukewarm. It wasn't cold or hot, and it was actually nauseating. Although the Lord rebuked these people, He also told them to "be zealous and repent."

He constantly gives us a chance to turn away from this lukewarm lifestyle. The question is, will we recognize it and repent or live for years like this? My body started to strengthen, and so did my mind. We wanted to buy a house since we were living with my husband's mother for nearly three years. The door kept shutting, whether it was because we wouldn't agree on a home, the house we agreed on would sell, or I was too sick to look. Money wasn't an issue at this point because Timothy had been working a solid job at a power company in the area, and he was raising up the corporate ladder. I remember looking at new construction homes, saying, "This is my dream home," or thinking, *This is what I need to be satisfied.* I also missed and yearned for having my own home. The time we were to be with family was only supposed to be six months.

Unexpected circumstances are probably the hardest things we have to face as believers—bombs that come from absolutely nowhere. A car accident, finding out that your spouse is cheating on you, a sickness, a miscarriage, that unexpected phone call—you name it—we've all been through some kind of surprise. Jesus didn't promise us an easy life. In fact, in the book of James, it says, "Consider it pure joy whenever you face trials of many kinds." The Bible doesn't say *if* you face trials, it says, *whenever* you face trials. I didn't see what was ahead of me or what God would ask us to do; but He began to unravel the story one step of obedience at a time. Sitting in a hot tub at my parents second home in Arizona in the spring with my husband, there was this sense of a shift coming and being springtime. I knew it was time for new beginnings. Suddenly, we felt the Lord say to stop striving in trying to buy a home; but instead, He spoke to us, saying, "Sell your possessions." What? Why in the world would we do that? We had many of our belongings in storage and in the basement of our mother's house. Nevertheless, we knew we had to obey. I put up our baby things on online garage sales. Within minutes of posting them, I received messages saying there was interest at the price I was asking for. Dozens of baby and toddler items, including lots of clothes, would sell right away. Then as I started to think about the furniture we had, my mom told me she would buy it off as their furniture was extremely old. This seemed too easy. Timothy had a few hobbies, saltwater aquariums, and tropical fruit trees, especially figs. I was listing items in lots as I didn't have time to sell one thing at a time being sick and having a baby and a toddler. At one point, I counted Timothy's fruit trees. They were over one hundred, including fig cuttings. I thought to myself, *Who in world is going to want tropical fruit trees in freezing, upstate New York? Well, might as well put them all up on an online garage sale to see what happens!*

Father's Day weekend, I listed the fig trees and received huge response. I was shocked and overwhelmed with all the messages I received from people wanting to come and buy fig trees! We decided to have everyone come in a few evenings so we would not have to waste our time with selling one here or one there. At one point, cars were up the entire driveway (about one hundred yards long), and they had to take numbers because there was a line of people! Initially, I told Timothy, "Let's have a 'buy one, get one free' sale" because of the number of trees we had and wanted to get rid of them. I wanted them gone, and gone fast. He said, "No, honey, let's just wait." After a period of a few weeks, they were all gone, even the few random tropical trees we had. One man told us he was about to start a restaurant and wanted a specific fruit vine that we had. And other one loved guavas and always wanted to grow them. Here I was, thinking, *How in the world is there a need for tropical fruit trees in Northeast America?* To my dismay, there was, and Timothy and I remember chuckling to ourselves when the driveway was clear. The next thing was our car. Timothy had a Subaru a few years old. I know cars are harder to sell online and take more work, especially getting the price we wanted for it. In a conversation with a girlfriend, she said, "Wow, we have been looking for an older Subaru." A few days later, they were the new owners to our car. These are just a few stories of how easy it was to sell our things. There are too many more to write about; but when God is asking you to do something, and you don't understand why, it should be effortless. Striving was trying to buy a home; resting was selling our possessions.

There is a phrase called "kicking against the goads." Jesus asked Paul this question: "Saul, Saul, why do you persecute me? It is hard for you to kick against the goads" (Acts 26:14). Paul was killing and persecuting believers, yet God used him mightily for His kingdom after Paul realized He was, indeed, the Messiah. An oxgoad is basically a long stick with a pointed piece of iron on one end. The master of the ox, usually, is gently prodding, guiding, and steering the ox into the direction while it works to plow the fields. When a stubborn ox attempts to kick against the goad, this causes discomfort, and the ox will inflict even more pain by driving the pointed end into its flesh. This is exactly how trying to buy a house looked like for us. We didn't have His peace over it. It was stressful. We were fighting. We were striving. And it just didn't feel right, at all. We didn't realize, until later, that we just ended up giving up. Sin can do this as well.

If we are in any kind of rebellion in our lives, we are inflicting more pain upon ourselves. And stubbornness can do this too. We need to trust our Father in that. Like the ox might not know where it is going, it trusts its master to gently prod it where to go. If we don't trust our Master and think we can go about life without Him, we are hurting ourselves. This goes back to the conscience being seared. We can lose all of our senses and not feel anything anymore or become numb to the pain that is in our lives. He knows us so much better than we know ourselves, for He created us. Sometimes we need to let go and surrender so He can lead us into greener pastures or still, small waters. If we don't, then we'll stay trapped in a cage or cocoon and never get to experience the abundant, full life that God has for us!

My best friend from college was living in Australia, and her husband was the director at YWAM (Youth with a Mission). We were catching up on the phone and were sharing about what God was doing in our lives and that I was slowly starting to get better. Her husband very casually spoke and said, "Why don't you both pray about coming to Australia and doing a DTS (discipleship training school)?" He also suggested that if we were to do it, do it in September because there were parents leading the school, and normally they were young adults. Our children were one and three years old at the time. DTS was a three-month lecture phase about the foundational topics of God and a two-month outreach phase to third-world nations. It was June, so we would have to make a quick, huge decision. At first, we thought he was crazy. However, the more we thought about it, we decided to take it seriously and consider it. At this point, Timothy had a job of ten years, working at a power company in a managerial position. He was climbing the ladder quickly and was about to get a large promotion. We were in a position, financially, where we had a ton of freedom. We realized, however, that when we looked for a home, it wasn't working, and selling our possessions was (too) easy. All of a sudden, Australia came up randomly, whether it was on the radio, through a conversation, or just a fresh heart for the nation. I knew it was time to make a big leap and do something drastic. However, it took Timothy a bit longer, being the provider of the family and having a great job. He knew that if he were to walk away from the job, we would be walking away from financial security.

Back to Lana Vawser, I stumbled across her itinerary; and lo and behold, she was coming to America to speak and happened to be coming to New York about four hours west of where we lived! I almost fell off my chair when I realized the person who was prophetically speaking over my life was going to be in my state! We drove across the state of New York as all I wanted to do was personally thank her and give her flowers. We made a trip of it and visited Timothy's dad as he lives on the way and showed the children Niagara Falls. It happened to be July 4 weekend in a place called Buffalo. We showed up, and the church actually had childcare for the conference. It is extremely rare that churches have free childcare for conferences, so it was such a blessing to be able to bring them and have them taken care of so that Timothy and I could sit in and listen. Worship started, and God began to speak to Timothy about surrendering everything and going into the mission field. Then the pastor of the church came and had a similar message. To top that, Lana's message was about a season of moving physically and giving up everything. She said it was a season for drastic change and to trust God for the next big location change. It couldn't be any more confirming for us. The time of the initial phone call from our friend in Australia to this conference was about a month. Timothy and I looked at each other, and we knew, that day, we were going to make one of the biggest decisions of our life—to walk away from a secure job to go into the mission field. I thanked Lana, gave her flowers, and knew God used her again to make that decision. There wasn't too much discussion on the four-hour drive home. We were quite in shock yet had an unwavering peace.

It was not going to be easy to share this news with family. We were about to tell them that we were going to take their grandchildren to (literally) the other side of the world. It is crazy to quit an amazing job, take your children, and go to a foreign land, away from your friends and family. My parents actually did something similar but for a different purpose. They, of course, wanted to know how we would be able to take care of our family financially and didn't understand the concept of being supported by people and trusting God with all of our needs. We did not expect them to, but they handled the situation the best they could, and we respect and honor them for that. Timothy knew he had to tell his work and give them more than just a two-week notice. He arranged a meeting with the CEO of his company. He right away said, "I am leaving my position."

And he asked, "Why is that?"

Timothy said, "I am going into the mission field."

His CEO responded with such grace and said, "That a boy!" He shook his hand and told Timothy that he would be our first supporter. This response was amazing. He could have reacted totally differently, and we would have still done it, but it was definitely nice knowing we had not only his blessing but his support as well. As we started to tell our friends, we had a mix of responses—anywhere from them being not shocked at all to people thinking we were crazy. We didn't let the response of man shift our course. We were focused on the journey ahead and had to have a single-minded focus, which was Jesus. He spoke, and no matter what the reaction was from man, we could not change our minds because there was an unspeakable peace that followed our decision.

As the summer quickly went by, we kept selling possessions and raised enough money to pay for our lecture fees for school as well as health coverage and flights. It was definitely hard emotionally as we were leaving family and friends behind for a six-month commitment. We did not know in advance which third-world nation we would be taking our family to on outreach. What we did know was that God said to go and knew we were taking one step at a time. We did not know what would happen after the six months either, but we did know Timothy could not walk back into his work with the same job. We didn't quit a job and sell everything to go back to work six months later and come back into the same lifestyle. This was pretty hard for me as someone who is a planner and likes to know what the future is going to look like. It isn't exactly easy to live six months at a time. But there is something beautiful about surrendering your life to God, especially when He doesn't give you the two-, five-, ten-, or twenty-year plan. There is a lot of wisdom in the scripture: "Therefore do not worry about tomorrow, for tomorrow will worry about itself. Each day has enough trouble of its own" (Matthew 6:34).

There was a spirit of control in my life that I had to surrender. I never really had to surrender the area of finances or plan of my life to God because I always had security in those areas. My plan was to be a stay-at-home mom until my children were in school and then go back to teaching French. I never planned on getting an awful, debilitating sickness or living with family for three years, having a miscarriage, or being let go from my first teaching position, getting hurt from close friends, having to walk away from a ministry Timothy and I pioneered. The list could go on and on. The question arises: What do you do when you are faced with unexpected circumstances, when your character is tested? How do you treat the people around you? Do you get anxious, or do you have peace? I have failed many times in my reactions to different circumstances. I have panicked, cried, questioned God, felt like I was losing my mind, and have been short with my husband and children. There have been other times when I took the time to pray and talk to God. When we had our miscarriage, I cried a lot and remember speaking in tongues because I didn't have the English words for the grief when told my baby didn't have a heartbeat. I was never angry at God or more confused; but in this situation, I let it go and had the supernatural peace of God take over. Within forty-eight hours, I was healed emotionally and physically. That isn't normal to be completely okay after losing your first baby; but with God, all things are possible. And when I let go and trusted God that I would meet my firstborn in heaven one day, He somehow took that deep place of brokenness and healed it. I can't wait to meet that child in heaven!

I never thought we would be leaving upstate New York, let alone go to the nations. Did I have a heart for other nations and cultures? Of course. I had traveled to India, Europe, Canada, and the Caribbean. I was also always attracted to people who were in minority groups, maybe because I was, or I loved learning about someone from a different culture and background. I think it's something God put on my heart ever since I was a little child. Maybe it is simply because He is a lover of people and created nationalities and cultures. Timothy, too, always had that passion for people of different cultures as he was involved with many different ethnic college groups at the University of Kentucky. God was bringing us to Australia, to an international school where about a dozen different nations were represented. Then He would bring us to a third-world nation where we would be able to really taste a different culture and people group. He knows the desires of our heart; and if we are yielded to Him, He will give them to us! We didn't really see all this before we left but had a large anticipation of it.

August finally came, and we were weeks away from moving to the other side of the world. Timothy decided to work until the very last day (Friday, and our flight was Sunday). Our children didn't really understand what was going on, but their lives were about to change as well. It was funny because as a young mom, I really was adamant about their little schedules. My life mostly revolved around them. Although there is nothing wrong with having your children on a good schedule, we should not be controlled by them. And for me, I was controlled by the clock. Nothing ever got in the way of their perfect nap times because I needed to rest or get things done. I was very uptight with noise as well and wasn't really flexible on things like this. Maybe it was because I was very sick for the first two years of Priya's life, and I needed the rest; but little did I know, God was bringing me into a time of letting go. Packing for six months was not stressful as God was teaching me simplicity and having peace through situations that could be stressful when they actually were not. We said goodbye to family with tears and anticipation.

On the drive down to New York City to John F. Kennedy Airport, I had a peace once again that we were doing what God wanted us to do. It was a new season, and I was excited because my body started to finally get better. And although it wasn't perfect, it was well enough for me to travel and take care of the children again. We hopped on our first flight to LA and, six hours later, arrived in the middle of the night. Our two-year-old daughter, Priya, was just falling asleep as we landed, and I thought to myself, *Oh, this is going to be a long layover.* We were in line at Starbucks, and she had a complete meltdown. I am not talking about just screaming but on the middle of the floor with her legs flailing up and down, screaming at the top of her lungs. The nurse said to me after giving birth, "She has quite the vocal cords." When I heard the word colic, I got chills because she literally screamed for the first three months of her life. Little did I know, they'd still be at full strength at age two and to this day.

So there was a circle of people around her staring and then staring at us as her tired parents. In Timothy's loving yet strong way, he said to all of them, "What, you've never seen a crying child before?" He then picked her up and walked away. At the time, it wasn't fun. But now, looking back, I laugh. I think the days of people-pleasing were slowly coming to an end. There was an alert that came on our phones about a possible active shooter in the airport, and there was a lockdown. As much as my old nature was to panic, I didn't know how to anymore. After the few years of renewing my mind against worst-case scenarios, God turned worst-case scenarios into best-case ones. We prayed as we waited for our flight to Brisbane, Australia, and the Lord kept us in peace in the meantime. Priya finally calmed down, and we boarded on a Qantas plane for the longest flight we'd ever been on—fourteen hours. I could have added extra stress to myself by thinking, *How am I going to fly with a two- and four-year-old across the world?* I could have asked other moms what to do, but I choose to think of best-case scenarios and that it wouldn't be stressful at all. The children were absolutely amazing the whole way.

Chapter 11

HEALTH AND THOUGHT LIFE

Often in life, do thoughts come through the mind about past, present, or future situations? If you're like me, thoughts come all the time, and we need to filter them. Dr. Caroline Leaf was someone who I came across after I started to get better. God used her to confirm everything that God taught me when I was sick that, basically, there is indeed a correlation between our thoughts and our health. "Research shows that 75 to 98 percent of mental, physical, and behavioral illness comes from one's thought life. This staggering and eye-opening statistic means, only 2 to 25 percent of mental and physical illnesses come from the environment and genes" (Leaf, p. 33–34). When I first read this quote, I nearly fell off my chair. In my heart, I knew it to be true, but this statistic is absolutely astounding. She has done a lot of work on neuroplasticity and has studied the science between thought and health. She's done a great amount of research on this topic, and I recommend her book, *Switch on Your Brain*, to anyone, especially those fascinated with the topic of renewing their mind. I was awful at science in school; however, this book is quite easy to follow! She said, "Every morning when you wake up, new baby nerve cells have been born while you were sleeping, that are there at your disposal to be used in tearing down toxic thoughts and rebuilding healthy thoughts. The birth of these new baby nerve cells is called neurogenesis, which brings to mind, 'The Lords mercies… are new every morning' (Lam. 3:23)" (Leaf, 2013, p. 24) When I read this quote, so much hope was infused into my soul, not only because I have new baby nerve cells being born every night but that they are actually used to renew my mind. Dr. Leaf didn't say that at a certain age these stop growing. She mentioned in the same chapter, "According to Dr. Herbert, negative thinking leads to stress which affects our body's natural healing capacities" (p. 35).

I believe most of us can agree, if not everyone, including doctors, that stress is not good for your body. I know that when I am stressed, my chest tightens. I have more back pain and overall tension in my body. I have less self-control when it comes to things, like food, and maybe drink a bit more coffee, chocolate, or eat french fries. I might also check social media a bit more, which studies say, can be as addictive as drugs. God has given us prayer and the Word to go to Him when we are feeling anxious or stressed. Why go for a cheap substitute? It's like you're starving and all you want is a nice steak and potatoes, but instead you are given bread crumbs. Bread crumbs will never satisfy that hunger, and you'll keep wanting to eat more if that's all you have.

"You will keep him in perfect peace, whose mind is stayed on You, because he trusts in you" (Isaiah 26:3). This is one of my absolute favorite scriptures. It speaks of an amazing peace that we can possess. But there is a condition, our mind has to be stayed on Him. This doesn't translate to just thinking about God here and there, it is a constant thinking about God. There is also another condition—that we trust in Him. So the keys to having peace are thinking about God and trusting Him constantly. If we could just get that right, stress would have no place in our lives. I remember a time where my baby was screaming, and I was chasing my toddler from getting into things, and the symptoms were all manifesting. I made a cognizant decision to think about God and how much He loved me. Peace overwhelmed me to the point where the concept of stress became foreign to me. I came to a beautiful place of trust that I'll never forget and stayed there. I believe that because of that place in my mind, my body followed. It seemed that my mind was controlling my body when it was submitted to God and not the lies of the enemy. Again, truth over symptoms—even though the symptoms seemed so real, the unseen truth was more powerful. I was reaching a place of laughing at my symptoms as my faith strengthened.

As I was being made perfect in His love, authority started to grow in me. It was there all along, but I believe that I didn't have quite the revelation of Who I carried because I was too busy in fear and anxiety. I let the past dictate too much in my life. Those familiar spirits that had been in my generational line for thousands of generations were distracting me in the things that felt normal and real: depression, anxiety, fear, pessimism, and confusion. There is a beautiful thing about being a first-generation Christian, but it is also very pioneering in a sense that you are the first in generation after generation to find truth, and there is an enemy who is ruthless and goes straight for the jugular. In my case, he tried to take my life twice. My husband is also the first child to be Christian in his family. It is so amazing and a privilege to bring our children up in the Lord so that they can continue in the faith and pass it on to their children.

We landed in Australia and drove an hour north to a place called Sunshine Coast. We were in the spring season, and my sinuses were immediately filled. But I was too enamored by the beauty of Australia that I wasn't bothered by it. We were given a standard car for the duration of our stay. Where we lived was a very hilly area, and Timothy didn't know how to drive using a gear stick. The plus side to having jet lag is there is no one on the road when you can't sleep in the middle of the night. Timothy would take the car for a drive and just felt the pressure of trying to learn it so soon. We decided to make life a bit easier and find an automatic car. Our friend helped us find one for about fifteen hundred dollars. It was an old, red Toyota Camry with many dents. We didn't care about that, and it was humorous because we had a newer red Toyota Camry back in the States. What were the chances? Not very high. But I believe it was a reminder of God's faithfulness. We had a week before class started, so we had time to meet our school leaders, see our friends, and adjust to the time zone (a fourteen-hour difference).

This particular YWAM base hadn't seen a family do a DTS for over ten years. In general, YWAM is usually young, the staff and students are generally around the age group of eighteen to twenty-five. Thankfully, our school leaders happened to be parents of six children. Unbeknown to me, they had their staff team agree to take turns to watch our children. This enabled both Timothy and I to be present in class every morning, as well as an evening class once a week. With Elijah being four, this was my first break as a mom to have our children taken care of until lunch time and was an enormous blessing. When you're a mother of children under five and you go from watching them all the time to having three months of having Monday to Friday mornings off, it is quite a blessing! I am so grateful that they, and the staff, went out of their way to help us. They certainly hadn't signed up to watch children when they came in to staff for DTS. Twelve weeks of solid foundational topics like spiritual warfare, the Father heart of God, and identity really blessed me in so many ways. I wish I had gone through this when I was younger, but God obviously knew I needed to hear it at the age of thirty-three and provided a way for it! So not only did God provide childcare for my children, but also gave me the break I needed as a mom. In turn, I would be a better mother for them! They had never done anything like this before, so it was an enormous blessing for us. We, of course, were the oldest in our school as most of the other students were in that young adult age bracket. Since we've worked in young adult ministry for about five years, we felt very comfortable around them and adjusted well. We both met with mentors weekly; had homework and personal journals; and shared a house with two couples, one from America and the other from Switzerland.

There was one speaker that really influenced me; her name was Lael. Her topic was spiritual warfare, and she nailed it. Her teaching was a perfect mix of teaching in the spirit and in truth. There were times when she would just stop in the middle of class and point to different people and speak different words over them. There would be tears, healing, and restoration in the middle of class. The authority she carried was incredible. She knew Who was inside of her. I remember seeing a picture of her with a leaf blower, just blowing all the weeds away, and it felt like that is what happens when the enemy tries to get in her path and how easy it was to blow those leaves out of her way. She had full control over them, and all she needed was the leaf blower (or God) to be her strength and power. She would walk back and forth in the room, and the presence of God in her was so tangible, like when you meet a marine for the first time, and you see the strength he/she carries. You can even smell it; it's so strong. She gave some of her time praying over me in the afternoon while the children took a nap. God continued to heal really deep places in my heart. Her character and love matched her gifting, which really stood out for me! She taught that we fight from a place of victory, not for it; and there is quite a difference. I know this is a common phrase, but it's like peeling layers of an onion until you find some roots. There can be much crying and not a fun process to go through. But if we never deal with the root in our lives, we'll never find full healing.

Jesus is always willing to take us through the journey, but we need to also be obedient to the process, whatever that may look like. You know that they are the toughest of the tough and have been through some serious challenges in life. Take David Hogan for example. He has dedicated his life to preaching the gospel in Mexico. He has been shot in the head (and survived), bitten by venomous snakes (and survived), has prayed over countless people with various illnesses (and they have been healed), and has raised many from the dead (through Jesus), and most of his family members had been in situations where demons took control of their bodies. People like this are people the enemy does not want to mess with. After being a believer now for almost twenty years, I have found that the warriors in the faith have spent a lot of time in the trenches. Many people in the body of Christ can get taken out of the battle if they either stop fighting or give in to it. Some people will simply believe a lie, like "why would God do this to me if He actually loved me?" There are two lies within this common thought. God never inflicts sickness or trials on people, and He always loves His children. Some people have the belief that God caused a sickness to teach a lesson or cannot comprehend why a loving God wouldn't just heal straight away a person who is sick. I had similar thoughts in the beginning of my sickness journey but knew I truly had to take that thought captive because it was a lie of the enemy. Some other ones can sound like, "if God loved me, He would heal me," or "if He was good, He wouldn't allow me to lose my job." There are so many examples that can be inserted here, but I think you catch the drift. God loves us no matter what comes our way. He is always good. There should be no *if* or conditional statement. His love or goodness does not shift according to our life circumstances, but our life circumstances shift based upon His goodness and love. If we focus on foundational truths like this and what the Bible says, we can be going through the hardest trial of our lives. But if our focus is on Him, He has the ability to shift any situation or circumstance. "But seek first His kingdom and righteousness, and all these things will be given to you as well" (Matthew 6:33). I started to get better, not when I was focusing on being healed and treating God like a genie in a bottle but when I was more focused on His love for me and relationship. We seek His heart, not what He can give us. He takes everyone on a different journey. Mine won't look like everyone else's. He knows us best, so He can make our journey specific to what we need the most in order to thrive and have the abundant life He has called us to have.

God also gives us the free will to surrender and be obedient. If surrender and obedience are His love languages, then control and disobedience are what He despises. There are scriptures to back this up all through the Bible. It takes a real fear of the Lord to walk in surrender and obedience regularly. There have been too many times in my life where I was disobedient, some of them where He asked me to give up coffee for a season or asked us to step away from ministry for a few months and focus on the family. These are just two examples, and again, maybe in both examples, I didn't understand why at first, but after being obedient, I realized the reasons. The first being, I was addicted to coffee, and He wanted to make sure I came to a place where I didn't need it anymore; and the second, there was a short period of a few months where I put ministry above my family, and my children were feeling it. My conviction has always been that I never want my children feeling like they are second to ministry because if they do, they will resent ministry and possibly even God.

I do not want to live with that. After about six months of focusing on family and getting things right on the home front, ministry came from a much healthier place and balance. Maybe it is simple obedience, like picking a piece of garbage up at the beach (I've done that), which isn't yours. If He can't trust us in the little things, how in the world will He be able to trust us in the bigger things?

Jesus went on a fast for forty days. Satan questioned God's authority in saying, "If you were the Son of God, tell these stones to become bread." The enemy has a way of questioning His authority and His truth. He is all about undermining and attacking identity. He uses our weaknesses to try and have us to believe a simple lie. The problem is, if we believe a few simple lies, they can really dictate the course of our lives. I know for a fact that if I had held onto a few lies when I was sick, I would not have become better. I probably would have prolonged my sickness if I actually believed Lyme disease is something you have for the rest of your life, or maybe God will heal me one day instead of proactively believing I am already healed, and being sick isn't my identity. It's all about making sure our minds line with the word of God when they are a little off of the truth. If a train goes a little off the track, will it still reach its destination? No, it will go further and further from the original track it was on and never reach the end.

Chapter 12

A FINANCIAL MIRACLE

John 15 states that apart from God, we can't do anything. It is so important that we take this into serious consideration. It goes on to say that "He cuts off every branch that bears no fruit" and how "no branch can bear fruit by itself." I think many times in our walk with God; we go through the day not reading the word, not praying, or even thinking about Him at all. It can be easy to get into the complacent pattern for days, months, and even years. This is a scary place to be because John 15:6 says, "If you do not remain in me, you are like a branch that is thrown away and withers; such branches are picked up, thrown into the fire and burned." It goes onto say, "If you remain in me and my words remain in you, ask whatever you wish, and it will be done for you" (verse 7). So there is a stipulation or condition on Him answering our prayers; it's remaining or abiding in Him. Will He answer the prayers of nonbelievers, or ours sometimes, if we are backslidden? Yes, I do believe so, out of His grace and mercy. But He goes on to say, "If you keep my commands, you will remain in my love, just as I have kept my Father's commands and remain in His love" (verse 10). You are my friends if you do what I command (verse 14). Again, there is a condition there. God loves obedience. Isn't it the best feeling in the world when you ask your kids to do something, and they just do it, don't question, and fight you; but they acknowledge you and obey right away? In most third-world countries I have been in, I see the behavior of children, and I marvel at how well-behaved they are and how much respect they have for their parents. Maybe it's the way they are disciplined, the lack of technology they possess, or the lack of toys they have compared to us as Westerners. I don't know, but what I do know is God has the secrets of parenting in the supernatural, and as much as I encourage parenting books, I mostly encourage the most a relationship with the Father who created children. He knows exactly the tools you need, specifically for your children (if you are a parent), so they grow up to have a thriving, abundant life!

Back to the story! There was a time during early lectures where we were presented the different nations we could go to on outreach. Some of the options were Uganda, South Africa, India, Japan, and Philippines. I remember them being presented to us and then told we had five minutes to pray and decide. Five minutes to decide where we wanted to take our family for two months seemed crazy, but at the same time, I do believe that sometimes the Lord speaks quickly, and this time we didn't really have a choice! They said we could write three options down in the order that we thought God wanted us to go. For me it was easy. Well, I am from an Indian nationality, so of course God wants me to go there, so it will be number one! Also, of course as a mother, I have to think about our children. I have already been to India many times, so I know I don't need to worry much about different illnesses like malaria or hepatitis A. The word "safe" was all I could think of, and it made complete logical sense. South Africa sounded nice, and from what I know, it is somewhat more Westernized. So South Africa became choice 2 and Japan sounded nice, so that would be choice 3. I presumed on this and did not allow God to speak. Timothy and I didn't talk about it before we wrote the nations out, but it did become a rough conversation afterward!

Timothy had put Uganda/Tanzania as number 1. That wasn't even on my top 3! I was getting upset. But somewhere deep inside of me, I knew fear was one of the reasons I didn't put Uganda/Tanzania on my list. I wasn't completely better from the illness, and my immune system was still weak. The last thing I wanted to do was put my body at risk and my children at risk. I hadn't surrendered this to the Lord and made my decisions solely based on fear. At one point, I said, "I will take one child to India, and you can take one to Africa." Obviously, I wasn't thinking logically if we were going to be away from each other for two whole months. The Holy Spirit was definitely stirring me on the fact that I made my decision completely based on the flesh and not Him. Timothy and I were having a rough night, but we slept on it, and both agreed to be open and continue to pray.

We met with our school leaders the following morning. Thankfully, our school leaders had a family, so they understood our battle. They were also completely aware that I was still recovering from an illness. Their daughter, at the time, was battling leukemia and (long story short). She was miraculously healed. I remember Dave (the school leader) looking at me and saying that he felt that we were supposed to go to Uganda/Tanzania. I told the Holy Spirit I would be open to what he had to say, knowing that I made this decision in my flesh, I knew I had to submit to both my husband and his decision. Was it easy? Not at all. But letting go and trusting God with a decision like this was freeing. I know I talk a lot about obedience and surrender even when its hard and we don't understand. This was yet another time that I had to trust God with my body recovering and our children. There is something exciting about surrendering an area of life to God that is really hard. I felt peace and knew God had something amazing for us there. Soon after that conversation, our children had to have a lot of vaccines, especially because we were going to Africa. I remember my son getting up in the middle of the night and throwing up blood. I actually didn't panic and knew it was a reaction from the vaccines. It only happened once, and he woke up fine. God gently reminded me that I entrusted them to Him. It's not a one-time occurrence where you do a baby dedication in front of a crowd; it is a daily act of prayer and trust.

Some of the ministry we were going to do in Africa was to preach the gospel, perform dramas or skits, teach, share testimonies, and spend time in the slums. Basically, if you had any fear of public speaking, this was not the outreach team you wanted to be on because we would do four crusades each week for about six weeks.

Most other teams would do more mercy ministries, such as visit orphanages, hospitals, or help build houses. Even though there were ten of us, we'd all have to share something at least once or twice per week. If anyone had a fear of public speaking, it was me. I remember during my school days, I would be absent when I had to do an oral presentation or get so nervous that I would stop talking in the middle and almost get a panic attack. I loathed any and every time I had to get up in front of the class. I also wasn't a Christian yet, so I didn't have God at the time to help me through this experience. I did teach French to middle school students for a few years after university. This wasn't nerve-racking to me because it was teaching children; I was not in front of adults. At my bridal shower, I didn't like being the center of attention at all, even opening up gifts in front of people was hard for me. God had a plan. But at the time, I was completely unaware.

Before going into our time to Africa, I want to share one of the most amazing testimonies of my life. Going back to our DTS, we had our lecture fees covered from selling possessions but did not have the twenty thousand dollars needed for the four of us to go on outreach. This would cover flights, visas, health coverage, food, housing, travel, and other fees. Our outreach leaders were very patient and gracious with us and would ask us regularly if we had the money yet. Every time, we said no. This lasted almost the entire three-month lecture until five days before our flight to Africa. We assumed the money would come in from our friends in America while we were in Africa until that sum amounted to $25,000 over the course of a few months. Our school leader mentioned plan B option in case the money didn't come in and that we had other options if we didn't go to Africa to still be able to complete the school in the future. In my heart, I didn't feel peace about it and stood on the passage from Philippians 4:19: "And my God will meet all your needs according to the riches of His glory in Christ Jesus." I also heard God say in prayer that He is a provider and will meet all our needs then saw a picture of me holding His hand. There were two mountains we were facing at the time (sickness and finances). I saw Him just flick the mountains out of the way with ease. The key was me holding on to

His hand. I made the decision in my heart that we were still going. Meanwhile, Timothy was in prayer and felt strong peace that we were going to be able to go to Africa, and there was to be no plan Bs. We made a video for our friends back in America. It was a challenge to our friends to consider giving $1,000 toward reaching the people in Africa. We assumed the money would come in from our friends in America while we were in Africa. A day later, we received an envelope from a YWAM missionary couple, saying, "We accept the challenge" with 2,000 AUD enclosed. I was amazed. Let me just make this clear for those of you that might not understand. Missionaries raise 100 percent of their support. Their salary is based upon faith and people giving to the Lord's cause. They said they saw a picture, and that basically it was a drain being unplugged, and God was going to use their money to unclog the drain for finances to start to flow for us. Little did they know, that picture would come to pass only five days later.

Monday morning came, the start of the last week of school before we leave for outreach on Sunday. If we didn't come up with the ground fees immediately, we couldn't go on outreach. There is a cafe in the church where the YWAM base is, and students would have coffees from there all the time. Timothy and I don't really use it because of the lack of money we have. I had this tug on my heart to get two drinks from the cafe for Timothy and I. Specifically, the Holy Spirit said, "I want you to use these as celebration for the provision for Africa." I was rather surprised but just obeyed. I handed the coffee to Timothy and said, "God told me to get these in celebration of the provision for our trip."

He said, "Did money come in?"

I said, "No."

As we sat in class, Timothy's mind pondered whether we really needed to spend much-needed resources on coffee. (He didn't know I used two gift cards another student gave us.) As he prepared to drink his final sip, the Holy Spirit spoke to him and said, "Why are you thinking with a poverty mindset? What is the cost of a cup of coffee to Me [God]? Everything on this earth belongs to Me!" As the words sank into Timothy's heart, he suddenly realized his error in letting the enemy have a voice. And with a new mindset, he raised his cup and thought, *This is to celebrate the funds coming in to go to Africa!*

Our outreach leader said she needed to speak to us during lunch. We both knew she was going to ask for the money again. With an extremely serious look on her face, she handed us a letter. It said, "I just wanted you to know that God told me to give you $20,000 so you can rest assure that you are going on this trip. God is behind you and before you. Love you so much! Love, anonymous brother or sister in Christ" I started to pinch myself and slap my face to make sure I wasn't dreaming. Timothy and I were both in complete shock. We were both speechless and just gave each other a blank stare. This was one of the best days of our lives as heaven and earth collided, and God showed up mightily. We were in shock for the rest of that day. Did I mention that this was given to us by a fellow missionary?—$20,000, the entire amount by one person (who doesn't have a salary).

God is a God of miracles. He is Jehovah-jireh (the Lord Who provides). We believe the word over our circumstance. Faith is not easy sometimes. But when God surprises us, it just is another reason to fall to our knees. May we never lose our wonder. This was the beginning of trusting God financially for us. We took a major step of obedience walking away from a ten-year job and financial security to entering the mission field, and God came through. The testimony spread throughout the YWAM base, and others who didn't have their outreach money were encouraged. It also led others to give money to us. It indeed was that plug that needed to be opened for provision to come. This miracle really spread back in the states too. Friends and family were in complete awe as they had never heard a story like this before in their lives. They were also encouraged because some of them were skeptical of our decision, but this confirmed that we were doing the right thing and in God's will. One of the best things about working in a major mission's organization is seeing the generosity in missionaries. This was all new to us at the time, and we never had experienced or met so many generous people. They all don't get a consistent paycheck or mostly any kind of extra money outside of living costs, yet they give every time there is an opportunity to give.

Once our base, about 150 missionaries, gave $52,000 in about 10 minutes to reach the nation of Pakistan. On a Sunday, most offering/tithe buckets don't bring in more than a few thousand dollars from a congregation of the same number or more. This really astounded me, and both Timothy and I have started to walk in generosity, so much more. It is such fun to give, especially when it is in the secret place and not in front of man because God knows our motives and in which motive we give from. He is the judge and lover of our souls, and He loves a cheerful giver (2 Corinthians 9:7).

When it comes to money, before having this revelation of generosity, I definitely was more tightfisted. Even when we were both working earlier in marriage and making a decent amount of money and had way more money than we do now, we were more frugal. To be completely raw and honest, we had many missionary friends in our earlier years of marriage who would ask or not ask, and we didn't give. It was only a few years before we left to do our DTS with YWAM when we started to be obedient to God in giving our finances. Now, though we raise 100 percent of our salary and still have no clue how we've made it three years in the mission field with trips to Uganda, Brazil, India, and Pakistan, I wonder if He just puts money in our account. I know it sounds crazy, but we know how much we get from our support and what our bills are, and those numbers aren't close at all. Not only that, but we have been able to travel as a family so much. My parents came to visit us in Australia, and their plan was to visit the South Island of New Zealand at the end of their visit. Being in Australia for a few years, we had always wanted to go to New Zealand, but the costs were too high. They had rented a two-bed house in a place called Wanaka on the South Island. I was thinking we could take that other room if we could fly there cheap. So I looked into flights, and I found airfare for the four of us, a round trip for $400. Usually, it is at least around $300 per person. When I told my parents, they agreed to not only pay for our airfare but for our rental car as well. Not only that, the cheap flights were on the exact dates my parents were going. God works outside of our little boxes. For a type A planner personality like me who thrives on a schedule, I've been quite humbled. Why plan out your life when every day can be a fun adventure with God where we have no agenda, only Holy Spirit as our guide?

The process leading up to the miracle of that $20,000 wasn't exactly seamless, but it wasn't exactly stressful either. We had instruction from the Lord to do this DTS, so just because we weren't sure how that money was going to come in, we knew that we had a word from the Lord to do this school. Because of my journey with Lyme, it truly, truly helped me not to stress out in situations like this. I learned how to not just know scripture but believe it with all of your heart. Philippians 4:19 was my forefront: "But my God will supply all your need according to his riches in glory by Christ Jesus." There are many scriptures on His provision, but I stayed with this one. Every time, the enemy would whisper, "You're not going on outreach," or "That amount is too high, it is never going to come in." He is always trying to put doubt into our minds, which of course is the opposite of faith. I knew enough that I couldn't feed doubt because if you feed the lie, you give it power. Timothy and I would, of course, be used by the enemy to try and discourage each other in the journey. It was a roller-coaster journey, but He was absolutely faithful in the end and kept His promise. On another note, God had asked us to make some financial decisions that made no logical sense, especially before going on outreach. They were hard to make. But again, submission is everything to Him. God's economy is completely different to ours. His numbers never make sense or add up, especially when it comes to giving.

Three years in the mission field, we didn't think twice about paying for someone's coffee or dinner as the Lord leads. God calls us to generosity. It is His heart. He has all the money in the world and wants us to lavishly experience the blessing of giving to others out of a joyful heart. I am thankful for the journey with YWAM as it has taught our family so much about this. After getting the money and realizing that we were going, we went shopping for items like mosquito domes, sleeping bags, bug spray, and whatever else we would need for Africa. Also, when you go with a team of people, you really need to pack light, especially because in these third-world countries, the vans aren't made for a ton of weight. When you're going as a family with children, packing light isn't easy. But thankfully, it was going to be warmer temperatures. We were told to take just a backpack and a carry on. I remember spreading Priya's diapers throughout the team. There was so much anticipation and fear mixed together. Remember, we were in our thirties, and our outreach leaders were in their low twenties. Our team was also young. We were about to spend two months with eighteen- to twenty-five-year-old singles. Let the story begin!

Chapter 13

Africa

We flew with Emirates for the first time into Dubai. It was probably one of the nicest, if not the nicest, airline I've ever flown. Flying with our four-year-old son wasn't too bad, but our two-year-old toddler was certainly not easy. Africa is about a one-day flight from Australia, and all parents can say that there is no taking breaks/naps on airplanes or layovers unless your kids are perfectly both synchronized in their sleep. I remember arriving there exhausted but with plenty of excitement. We drove almost three hours in a van with our team to the village we were staying in. We were able to rest one day and then start ministry the next. There are no car seats or even seat belts in Africa. Priya would have to sit on our lap, and Elijah sat tight next to us. I remember all the mosquitoes that were everywhere, allowing fear to sink in. They all don't carry malaria, but some do. We were told to wear long sleeves in the early morning and evening with bug spray. Our team decided not to take the malaria medication but to be cautious as to what the locals had to say about what to do on the practical side of things. I especially did not want to take it because I was on it for months on and months off when I had the Lyme disease and saw how it affected my body. We slowly adjusted to cold showers and had to adjust to going to the bathroom squatting down. The children adjusted a lot quicker than we did. They are so much more adaptive than we are, and traveling with them wasn't nearly as hard as we thought it was going to be.

We went to a village to set out for our first crusade ministry. We had no idea what to expect but were so excited. We drove on bumpy dirt roads feeling a bit nauseous but thanking God for the opportunity to serve Him. I realized I had to leave my Westernized comfort at home. I think, going to a third-world country for an extended period of time really is a check on how dead you are to yourself. I could have had the mindset of, "This is awful. I am about to take cold showers, go on a squatty potty, and have mosquitos on me constantly." Or I could say, "Lord, this is a season where I can serve You wholeheartedly, where my comfort has nothing to do with it, and don't want anything to get in the way of hindering that with You. Basically, I never want 'self' to stand in the way of serving You, no matter what that looks like."

I remember being in Africa every day waking up to His peace as I allowed myself to "go with the flow" and not be so tied to my children's schedules. Mealtimes were later than normal with breakfast starting around ten o'clock, lunch around three o'clock, and dinner around eight o'clock. We couldn't just take a car to the grocery store to get snacks but had to be flexible and adjust to the team. We even had to have water sparingly. We were in a situation where we had no control and really had to trust God at times with not only basic needs but also a few times with our lives (I will share later). In the places we would stay, I would just pray we would be able to have our own room. We had but usually had to share one bathroom with a team of ten of us. One of the bigger adjustments was trying to keep the children quiet, especially when they would wake up a few hours before the rest of the team. When it came to ministry, we would often switch but at times bring them with us. There were many late-night crusades where the kids would pass out in the van. Also, there were times when we had to really old on to and keep watch over them at night because of being scared that they would be taken away as they are *muzungu* (white skinned). Well, technically, they aren't completely white but half white. In their eyes, however, they are *muzungu*. The culture actually believes the *muzungus* have more power.

Even some of the Christians believe that the White Christians have more power than they do.

My husband brought one of the local kids up to the front and asked him to help pray for the sick so that he could try and teach that this is a lie and not the truth at all. Lies sometimes can be embedded in cultures for generations. This is why, even among the Christians, their cultures can speak louder than God. Personally, in my culture, being academic is strong. I've seen Indian Christian parents push academia on their children. Status can still hold power, and I believe this is from generations of what caste you are from. There are Brahmans at the top and untouchables at the bottom. There is much bragging in my culture of "what does your son/son-in-law do?" Parents would love to say, "Oh, he's a doctor or manager." Let's just say, it wasn't good when I first told my parents Timothy was leaving his managerial position to become a missionary.

Shame is a huge thing too of Indian culture. If a child brings shame to their family, they might be disowned or even killed. Money is a large aspect, too, of Indian culture, and people are treated differently according to their job status. I've always hated this as a believer. I saw myself doing this a little when I had my masters or, even more so, when Timothy got his MBA degree from a great university or when he got upgraded at work. I caught myself saying, "Where is my heart in this situation? Am I bragging or trying to gain the approval of man?" So this is a generational, cultural stronghold that I had to sever with because, now that I am a Christian, none of that should matter. I am a child of God, and it doesn't matter what my or my husband's title is. I have a relationship with God first and foremost, and from that, whatever worldly title I have doesn't even matter. It is almost like an identity question. "What do you do for work?" Then you get associated with everyone in your position. Or "What nationality are you?" and you are automatically associated with an ethnic person they know who is of that same nationality.

How many of us generalize that if you know one person from one background, everyone else in that same background is the same? There have been so many times where someone asked if I knew their Indian friend from Texas or California just because I was Indian too.

I think people try to find who they are and their identity so hard because it's something God created us to find in Him. Apart from Him, we don't really have a purpose or identity in life. If we haven't found the One we were created to live for, we walk around aimlessly from high to high with no purpose, following emotion and feeling instead of doing what we were created to do: to find Him and then ask Him what our purpose is.

In Indian culture too, having a firstborn son is really important so that he can go to work and (eventually) provide for his parents as they age. I think this goes for many cultures. These were lies I really had to leave at the cross because once I was a new creation, my identity was now in Christ, not my job title, my birth order or gender in the family, or (even) my nationality. These all were laid out at the cross. Culture is a beautiful thing, but the values that come from culture should never surpass our faith because if they do, then we put ourselves in a place of compromise.

So back to Africa. Usually, before we would start speaking on stage, we would perform a powerful skit. I love them because they present the gospel message in such a powerful way where there are no language barriers. Everyone can understand just by watching. There were so many times that I was in tears when we would perform them because of how powerful they were. We did have someone briefly explain the drama, but I don't know if it was even necessary because they were all self-explanatory. I remember, it was the first night of speaking in front of a crowd and going back to public speaking. I was extremely nervous. But when I got on that stage, for some reason, speaking in front of the Ugandan people didn't seem nearly as intimidating as speaking in front of Westerners. They were so joyful, hungry, and full of anticipation. It seemed as if this spirit rose up inside of me with excitement, and I started to share my testimony of how I became a Christian out of Hinduism. Usually, people listen to a story like that because it isn't the norm; and thankfully, God is glorified by it every time. The nervousness suddenly went away as I started to share, as my focus rose to thinking about glorifying God over speaking to a crowd. The story was encouraging me because what are the chances that God moves my parents from India to America, and then my sister and I became believers? I remember getting on my knees at one point and just sharing the story from there because I was in such awe and humility from Him. I walked off the stage, and the next person on the team got up to share the gospel. It was a powerful night of salvations, miracles, and healings, and it seemed like we weren't even trying. There is power in hunger and humility, and these people were so open. It was so beautiful as we were able to lay hands on them and minister freely.

The next day, we would do door-to-door ministry where we would go down the street and share the gospel with people as we felt led by the Spirit. Once where we shared with about ten people, nine of them would say yes. It seemed way too easy. So many thought of trying to do this in America, but most people wouldn't even give you the time of day for a few minutes. I think it is hard to see the desperation in a first-world nation when everything is at your fingertips from having access to health insurance and hospitals, to clean water and food, to having drive-throughs and fast technology. There are too many luxuries that we take for granted; and sometimes, I believe, they can be a complete hindrance to our hunger for the things of God. The enemy loves to distract us. One of his tactics is to not only get our eyes off Jesus but also to make us think we can somehow live this life without Him. If he gets us to believe this lie, we can go days, weeks, months, years, and decades without having a relationship with Him. We become cold and stagnant and cease being like Christ. We wonder why sometimes the world wants nothing to do with Christians? Because they might not see a difference in our lives versus the lives of nonbelievers.

We invited the people we met to the crusades we were running that week. We saw a lot of them show up and be transformed by the gospel message. We ran crusades at night and preached in jails, taught in churches, and ministered in many different ways during the day. We were transitioning to Kampala (the main city in Uganda) for another ministry. We were invited to speak at a crusade where there were going to be over five thousand people. It was a Christmas outreach, and the pastor we were working with was the biggest gospel singer in the country. We went to his house with our team, and he looked at us and said, "This family is staying with me." So we had the honor of staying in his guesthouse and were able to get to know his children and him a bit better. The crusade night came, and most of the team were nervous to share because of the size of the crusade. The leaders asked me to share my testimony, and I wanted to say no. But something was screaming "yes" inside of me. They told me I would have ten minutes. The locals went on to say I had five, then one minute. One? How was I supposed to share my testimony in one minute? The event was so big; they had it all planned out but wanted to squeeze us in as we weren't originally part of it. At this point on outreach, I had only spoken a few times in front of people. Our team performed a powerful skit. Something about the excitement of the crowd overwhelmed me, and again, God gave me a vigor and lion-like confidence as I (quickly) shared how God found me. We were used to having translators; but because this was a major city, we didn't need one. I was used to having a few seconds between each line with translators, but I had to think fast and get right to the point. As I shared the power of Christ, the crowd cheered at various times. The pastor later told me that I should have done an altar call, but I wasn't being sensitive to the Holy Spirit and was probably too scared that we didn't have enough time for that. Of course, I regret this; but life is all about learning from your mistakes!

Just a few days following the crusade, I started to feel a little nauseous. I got tested for malaria, but it came back negative. The nausea turned into vomiting and diarrhea and being uncontrollable. We had to go to a hospital. When I say hospital, I'm talking about a bush hospital in the middle of nowhere. I got tested, and it looked like I had a terrible form of E. coli. They said, it was the worst they had ever seen. I remember blacking out at various times and not being able to even make it to the Squatty Potty just outside the hospital. Timothy was scared that this was going to be it for me. I was then pumped with antibiotics and liquids and couldn't hold anything down for close to forty-eight hours. Our wonderful outreach leader looked after our children. We were supposed to be leaving for Tanzania in the next few days but had a feeling I wasn't going to be able to get on a plane. The amazing thing about African culture is their positive outlook on life. The nurses would speak so much life over me. I remember them worshipping and saying, "You will be well." God was speaking to me in the midst of being ill and told me to take note of their words. It was almost as if they were prophesying over me. Because I was sick before, I knew that any lies of death, lasting illness, or anything negative, I shouldn't even entertain. The only truth I would entertain was that I was going to get better and get better quickly. I was not going to stay stuck on the idea that I was in the middle of nowhere in a bush hospital with nurses and doctors without appropriate degrees. Ultimately, God was taking care of me, not them. I slowly started to eat rice and bread and regained enough strength to go back to the pastor's home. I was feeling so tired from the medication when, all of a sudden, I got awful stomach pains. I knew I didn't want to go back to the hospital. Timothy wanted me to, but I knew all I needed was rest. We ended up canceling our flights so that I could have a few more days to rest. I slowly started to recover.

We rebooked our flights for later that week, and then all of a sudden, Elijah started coughing violently. I remember thinking, *What is this? I was just fighting for my life, and now my son is running a very high fever, and sounds awful.* Back to the hospital we went, and he ended up having a really bad respiratory infection. We had to fly the following day. We couldn't cancel our flights again. We took the medicine, prayed, and started driving to the airport. Elijah said he felt he wanted to throw up. I felt overwhelmed as we had a very bumpy hour-long drive to the airport. He said to pull over. We did, and he started to vomit. I believe it was from the medicine. I prayed that he would make it on the plane. Thankfully, the flight to Kenya was only about an hour. It felt like the longest hour of my life as our son was still running a high fever and just didn't look at all well. We immediately got him to the room we were staying and had him rest. The next day, he couldn't walk. So many things were going on in my mind; but again, I was choosing to not feed the fear and worst-case scenarios. It's not like we go through a test once. Satan does anything he can to bring this familiar spirit up; and for me, it was fear.

We prayed, had him rest, and thankfully, after a few more days, he started to get better.

It was a roller coaster of a week between my son and me both having awful experiences. There can be peace in the middle of the storm if we choose it. We only had a few weeks left of outreach in Tanzania, and I was able to speak about renewing our minds in Christ, and our team had one day to go on an African Safari. It was a beautiful way to close our trip. Although those two months were some of the hardest in our life, they stretched our capacity. I always tell people, outreach for us makes everyday life a lot easier. Regularly, there were surprise circumstances, events, and unexpected turns. We had to make decisions quickly as a family yet honor our young leaders at the same time. We learned to forgive and die to ourselves quickly. We stretched our comfort zone on many occasions but always made sure both children were safe.

Chapter 14

STEPPING INTO FULL-TIME MINISTRY

I remember our trip back to Australia. When you are on a team, and you work with a travel agent, you don't really have a say in your flights. When you fly with children under five, you want to get to your destination the quickest way possible with very limited layover times. Our itinerary going home was the nightmare itinerary for any parent. Somehow, we had five flights from Tanzania in Africa to Brisbane, Australia. A scripture came to mind when I first looked at the itinerary, and it was Matthew 6:34: "Don't worry about tomorrow for tomorrow will worry about itself, each day has enough trouble of its own." Do I obey this verse perfectly all the time? Not quite. But in this instance, I chose to. If I were to logically think this all out, I probably would have a meltdown and refuse to do it. To someone who is in the process of renewing their mind and overcoming anxiety, this flight itinerary was like a mother's worst nightmare.

After spending all day packing and wrapping up loose ends, we left Tanzania around 8:00 p.m. to drive to Kilimanjaro Airport, which was about an hour. Our flight was an early morning flight, so we decided to go to the airport in the evening so the children could sleep a while before the flight. Our first layover was six hours. After a bout of sickness and a trip to the airport clinic to get a malaria test, we were ready to check in. Our first flight left Tanzania around 4:00 a.m., and it was a quick one-hour flight to Kenya. This layover was two hours and then another quick flight back to Uganda. Then we had a seven-hour layover. We boarded our next flight to Dubai, and this flight was six hours. Following that, we had a five-hour layover. If you need to pause and get a cup of coffee, please do so because I am only halfway through.

Right before we boarded, what we thought would be our last direct flight, we heard an announcement that there would be a touchdown stop in Singapore. This would be a ten-hour flight. I thought that we would touch down, get passengers, and then fly out. This was not the case. We had a two-hour layover in Singapore, and we were greeted by everyone wearing masks. We were screened there over some kind of outbreak. Finally, we boarded our last flight to Brisbane, Australia, which would be the last five hours. We arrived in the middle of the night and spent about an hour getting our luggage and going through customs. But wait, we had to drive another one and a half hours back to the Sunshine Coast. We arrived there around 4:00 a.m. then unpacked to prepare a room to sleep in. In total, we had two van rides, five flights, five layovers, six countries, three continents, twenty-four hours in layovers, twenty-five hours in transit, totaling about forty-nine hours of straight traveling with very minimal sleep. How did the children do? Absolutely phenomenal. A few ten-minute meltdowns on a few flights and layovers, but it was so much better than I would have imagined.

Sometimes you wonder, how in the world did something like that go smoothly? And then you say, it was the absolute complete grace of God. We didn't use Benadryl once to give them so they would sleep on the flights to make it easier on us. After this, it seems like traveling anywhere is reasonably easy. Even flying from Australia to New York, which is at least a day of travel. I asked God to help me to stay calm during the traveling, especially when the children were being unruly, and my husband and I were not sleeping much at all. I believe anticipation is everything. It is all about the way that we think. Once I saw the itinerary, I could have started to stress, had anxiety, and literally gone to pieces. I could think, *Okay, I am traveling with children under five, am about to get no sleep, and try to and keep them quiet for that long a time in public.* I could have tried to express my anger at the travel agent and ask her if she knew I was a mother of young children, knowing she did, because she had all of our passports. I could have also taken it out on my team members who didn't have children because they didn't understand this itinerary would be very challenging. Or I could accept the situation and let go of the control and believe some simple truths in the Bible about not worrying and that He is with us wherever we go. All those things are possible for He who believes. And if I put Him first, everything else would fall into place. I could focus on how much He loves me and how much He wants to speak to me in these situations. I could (even) look for opportunities to look outside myself and our children, to tell the lost about Jesus.

It all boils down to, Where is your focus? What is your heart and mind set on? Is it me, or is it Jesus? This was a great test that, I believe, I passed with God's help. Do I pass them all? Certainly not. But when you obey, life is just so much easier than trying to do it on your own strength. Why strive when we can rest? Why even try to do life on our own strength when chapters in the Bible, like John 15, say we can't? Sometimes I think we make our life much harder than it has to be. This isn't what God wants for us. He wants us to not just know the Bible but to live it. What is the point of reading something, especially when it is the truth, if we aren't allowing it to transform us from the inside out? I can't live with head knowledge but desire to live with heart transformation.

We had a debrief week of saying goodbye to our classmates, adjusting to life back home (if we chose to go back), and for graduation. It was a stretching yet remarkable five months. Since we were on a six-month visa, we decided to stay in Australia one month to rest and pray for direction for the next steps. We honestly had no clue of what we were going to do next. All we knew was we wouldn't be going back to Timothy's job. We found a cheap Airbnb (the person who invented that actually went to my high school!) to stay in for that month and were able to get the rest we needed from being in Africa but also focus on praying for direction. Timothy and I were praying about what we thought God was saying for us next. We came together and felt the Lord was saying to come back and staff for two years. With YWAM, you usually give a two-year commitment, so I felt to come back on and staff with DTS, and Timothy felt he should be involved with a prayerhouse and help out with evangelism for DTS. There were other things, too, on our list, but those were the main roles. We talked with the base director, and he felt the same on his heart. Timothy went for a cup of coffee with our pastor in Australia, and something really incredible happened. Our pastor is a prophet. He has the office of a prophet. I believe there is a difference in being a prophet versus being prophetic. Without Timothy saying a word or even telling him we were praying for direction, he read Timothy's mind very specifically. He talked about us coming back and saw the word *prayerhouse* in gold letters over Timothy's head. If I were to write down everything he said, it would be a lot. But to sum it up, God used a prophet to confirm what He had spoken to us about direction. We spent that month together as a family, resting. It was a beautiful time as it was about to get busy in New York and as we knew we would have to spend the next six months' support raising a salary so that we could come back to Australia to staff with Youth with a Mission.

Everyone in YWAM supports, raises their entire salary, even the founder, Loren Cunningham. This isn't like most organizations where they require you to raise a certain amount, and then you are able to start in the mission field. They trust you and God to make a wise decision even if you do not have your full support once you start on the field. We didn't know if we could raise support in six months for the entire two years. It usually takes the average missionary about two years to raise the full support, so we had a daunting task and goal, but we were up for the challenge as we had seen God come through before. We had a flight from Brisbane to LA and then a quick flight to Tuscan, Arizona, as my parents had their winter home there, and my sister lives there as well. We thought we would spend a week with them and then fly back to New York. At this point, my health was much better. This was when I noticed I was beginning to feel normal again.

Getting to Tuscan, I was so excited to see my parents and sister and brother-in-law again. God did so much and was so excited to share all of this with them, not only on what He had done in my heart but about our adventures in Africa as well. For the first few days, the excitement and reuniting with them was beautiful. We told them about our journey and what was going to be next. It was hard enough to say goodbye to them for six months, but now we had to tell them that we were going to go back to Australia for a few years to be missionaries with YWAM. I wasn't really looking forward to this because, Christian or not, that is not easy news to tell the grandparents of your children. There may have also been an expectation of us coming back for good after six months, so in their minds, this might have been a temporary leave.

I remember their reaction and then all of a sudden getting familiar symptoms again. I knew there was a correlation to stress and allowing it to affect my body. I strongly did not accept the symptoms, never saying in my mind, "Oh, here we go again." Although the symptoms didn't go away right away, I knew in my hardest of hearts not to accept them or make room for them to be there. I was trying not to speak anything out loud to Timothy, such as "Here we go again" or "They never left." But a certain liar named the devil whispered, "See, God didn't heal you," and "See, you are going to be ill the rest of your life." Thankfully, I was able to rebuke the lie and stand in my healing even when the annoying flies came back to tempt me into fear again. Picture a lion getting harassed by flies. Do we see the lion cower in fear and think, *Oh, these flies are going to get me!* No! All the lion has to do is stand up and maybe give a little roar, and they just buzz off. It's very similar to how Satan tries to goad us as believers.

Chapter 15

BREAKTHROUGH

I always take the section in Matthew 4 about Jesus being tempted in the wilderness by Satan. He tries in the weak moments to throw a lie at Jesus. Jesus fasted in the wilderness for forty days and forty nights, and the Bible says that He was hungry. Now let me tell you, I've done a three-day water-only fast, and it was *hard*. I've known a few people to make it to forty days, and I really honor that they could go that long with the strength of God. So in verse 3, Satan says, "If you are the Son of God, tell these stones to become bread." So not only was he going after the fact that Jesus was hungry, but he was also trying to get Jesus to question His identity as God's Son. I have fasted in more recent years and have caved in, miserably, at the scent of food or after missing only a couple meals. Fasting really strengthens the area of self-control. This is a whole other chapter though! I recommend Mahesh Chavda's books on fasting.

So, Jesus replies in verse 4, "It is written: 'Man shall not live on bread alone, but on every word that comes from the mouth of God.'" So not only did Jesus come back with the truth (the word of God), but He addressed that we need spiritual food. The next lie from Satan was in verse 6 while Jesus was standing on the highest point of a temple: "If you are the Son of God, throw yourself down, for it is written: He will command his angels concerning you, and they will lift you up in their hands, so that you will not strike your foot against a stone." So now the devil saw that Jesus used the scripture and tried to use it against Him. He basically tried to get Him to commit suicide off a tall building. I would call this a "spirit of death." The last thing Satan tried to do was tempt Jesus with power. He took Him to a mountain and showed Him all the kingdoms of the world. In verse 9, he lied, saying to Jesus, "All this I will give you, if you will bow down and worship me," trying to tempt Jesus into worshipping him, and if He did, He would have all this power. Jesus had enough of Satan and replied, in verse 10, "Away from me, Satan! For it is written: 'Worship the Lord your God, and serve him only.'" After three lies that the devil came to Jesus with, he realized none of them were working. The last verse in the story read, "Then the devil left him, and angels came and attended him."

It's not that we are tempted because we are in Christ. If anything, we are a target, especially if we are living fully surrendered to God. If we are a threat to the enemy, he'll use our weakness to try and get us to stumble and fall. I've been there too many times and have fallen for the bait. The torment in my mind was literally 24-7. The problem is that I didn't know I was tormented in my mind or weak in that area. This is why we not only need to know the word of God but believe it with all of our hearts. If we don't, we will fall every time Satan tries to whisper in our ear. In Genesis, talking about the fall, the Bible says that "the serpent was more crafty than any of the wild animals the Lord God had made." He tempted Eve and questioned what God spoke to her about eating the apple with, "Did God really say?"

Isn't that a classic thought that can go through our minds? Does God really heal? Is there really only one truth? Other Christians do it, so it can't be wrong. What is once? God will just forgive me. Did he notice me? I could probably write a few novels on all the different lies that he has thrown my way and how they got me off course. The key is, not to let it in, and the best weapon is when we speak the word, out loud, against the lie. There have been so many times where I was walking down the street with my children or around people where I would either just randomly start speaking out loud or leave the room to remind Satan the authority of God's word. When Satan meant to torment me, after decades, I finally realized I can take that torment and use it as a springboard into God's truth. Not only did it sharpen me, but it grew me in the authority as the word was being spoken.

Second Corinthians 11:3 says, "But I am afraid that just as Eve was deceived by the serpents cunning, your minds may somehow be led astray from your sincere and pure devotion to Jesus." There is power in Paul's words here. How often do our minds get led astray from Jesus? I believe this is where the enemy first targets. *It's a simple thought like, Your husband doesn't love you. It's okay to flirt with another man. You deserve it.* Or *It's okay to just look. You're not cheating.* Here is yet another scripture talking about Satan: "He was a murderer from the beginning, not holding to the truth, for there is no truth in him. When he lies, he speaks his native language, for he is a liar and the father of lies" (John 8:44).

When people ask, What is your native tongue? They are referring to a language that has been exposed from birth, the language you grew up with, and is the most natural to you. Here in this scripture, it says, the devil speaks his "native tongue" when he lies, which is what he has been exposed to since birth, the language he grew up in, and the language that is most natural to him. When we speak our native tongue, we don't have to try or think about what we say because it comes to us naturally. In this scripture, it describes that he lies and speaks naturally without even having to try because he is the father of lies.

Imagine every word out of your mouth being a lie. You would speak lies to your children every day. You would tell them that the sky is brown, that the grass is purple, and that the bread they are eating is actually stone. You would tell them you aren't their parents, but you are their friends. You would tell them that fire is cold and knives are soft. Do you see where I am going with this? This would create utter confusion and chaos. Their minds would not only be confused, but then they would tell their friends the same things. The lies would spread, and they wouldn't know better because they are taught from a young age. So imagine the devil doing that to every person on earth, implanting lies into nonbelievers and believers alike. This is one of his main jobs to get us to believe the lie so that we are hindered from being fully obedient and surrendered to Christ. The problem is, once we believe a few lies, it can have a domino effect into believing many. Once the enemy sees we'll believe a few, he'll just throw us many lies at once, and our conscience will be so seared that he won't have to keep trying. Our minds have become filled with bitterness, envy, jealousy, lust, fantasy, darkness, and every evil thing. Dr. Caroline Leaf has studied that this can lead to Alzheimer's, mind fog, and other mental health issues. I allowed the devil to torment me for over fifteen years and really only became alive when I started to take every thought captive. From there, life can flow in and out of the mind.

So now, after a few symptoms lingering, we flew back to New York to share the news with family and friends. Again, when you tell your family that you are planning on moving to the other side of the world and take the children, the reaction can be hard. My children weren't near to being adults yet, so I was not able to fathom or understand but know it was an adjustment from seeing them regularly face-to-face to now only doing video calls. We've always lived close to family, so it was a shift for everyone to be away. We didn't have a place to stay for the few months we were going to be in New York and certainly didn't want to be in an Airbnb because, financially, we are trying to raise enough money to be full-time missionaries. A local church heard our story and happened to have missionary housing. It was a Presbyterian church that owned a two-bed apartment and was vacant at the time we were home. They said we could live there for no charge while we support raised. It was a miracle. Yet again, God came through at the eleventh hour. We were so thankful and especially moved by their generosity in this way as we were not members of their church. They barely knew us but were moved by our story, and they saw us as a family in Christ. It was a beautiful gift to us and one we will never forget.

As we started to support raise and meet with different people, we realized how daunting the task was of raising full support in six months. Our family usually goes to about one conference a year, depending on location, cost, and of course, who is leading it. We believe they are good investments to not only our ministry but to our personal walks with Jesus. This was one we've been to before called Power and Love. This was our third one in the past four years. They are led by Todd White whose heart is to speak about identity in Christ and then go out and show Jesus to the world. He does this simply by walking in the power of the Holy Spirit wherever He goes, knowing that He carries the Author of the universe inside of him. The typical stories are, he gets a word of knowledge (a specific word over someone) over someone's sickness or situation. He confirms it with the stranger then prays, and that sickness either gets healed or the situation resolved. For example, someone is contemplating suicide and has just told God that if He doesn't show up, he/she will take their life later that day. The Holy Spirit leads Todd to that person, and of course, lo and behold, Todd prophesies life over that person, and that person's life is saved. Another simple example is, someone is suffering with some chronic disease, like rheumatoid arthritis, the Holy Spirit shows Todd this, he confirms it and asks, "Do you have rheumatoid arthritis?" They say yes; he prays; and there's instant healing. Was it always this easy? No. He shared that he had prayed for ten people a day for about six months and didn't see any healing. He persevered however!

I want to state that I am not elevating Todd White at all. He's a human being, just like you and me. You might be thinking that is incredible, or that's impossible! Well, take heart because you can walk hearing God's voice in the same way! Sometimes it is just baby steps, talking to someone in line at the store, sharing with them God's love, or just asking someone how they are doing. God then begins to speak by a thought or a word, then in faith you share it out loud. Soon you are sharing with this person things that you would never know, but God knows. As I always say, it all boils down to surrender and obedience. Are you more worried about what people will think, or do you care more about God's heart toward mankind? As we are able to receive God's love, it becomes natural to pour that love onto others wherever we go. After all, we are the aroma of Christ.

The conference was free (because we've attended one before). The cost of the hotel, food, and petrol—we would have to come up with. We did not have to buy lunch because I had packed snacks, or someone gave lunch at the conference (more provision). I googled cheapest places to stay, including Airbnbs, and I found a motel for $300 for four nights. We brought our children to this one so we were close to the conference in case one of us had to stay back. I thought to myself, *$300 is a lot of money for a missionary to pay out.* When Timothy had his job, we didn't have to think twice about hotel costs. I said, "Lord, we believe You want us to attend this, so we are trusting you!" The second day of the conference, we were out at dinner, talking to people about Christ. Someone from the conference (who did not know us or our situation) handed me an envelope and simply said, "I believe God told me to give this to you." Of course, it was almost the exact cost of the motel. God is absolutely amazing. The more we step out in the faith, the more He shows Himself off to us and the rest of the world. He is our ultimate provider. God used this to show us not only to trust Him step-by-step but to obey when we don't see the provision yet.

In August, God told us to go back. We arrived in New York in March. A lot of people told us, including pastors, that we were crazy. We clung to God's word and moved forward with what we were doing. Getting monthly support was slow and definitely didn't go the way we had expected it would. Asking people for a hundred dollars a month seemed easy, but it wasn't. July came rolling around, and we had only raised about $400/month with a few people giving just once. I questioned everything. We questioned everything. Of course, we couldn't live on that as a family, what should we do, abort the mission and go back to work? We knew we were called, but our financial circumstances weren't lining up with the word of the Lord. I prayed about it, and the Lord showed me a scripture. It was in Luke 9 when Jesus sent out His disciples to share the gospel. There was a whole chapter in a book about that scripture and what it meant. What caught my attention, specifically, was in verse 3: "Take nothing on the journey—no staff, no bag, no bread, no money, no extra shirt." *What? God, does this scripture apply to us in this day and age? Is that wisdom? Can that really apply to our situation?* I believe the Lord was saying, in that moment, to trust Him. We didn't need to have everything figured out, and we shouldn't make decisions based upon worldly circumstances if we knew we were supposed to go. After the confirmation of the word, we decided to buy plane tickets, in faith, that He would provide.

We continued to support raise and speak at churches. I've been overwhelmed time and time again how much provision is met. God was showing Himself off through us, to believers and nonbelievers, and it is such fun! I had the opportunity to share at a group called FaithMoms. If anyone knows me personally, they know I love giving roses. I was asked to provide a sheet with information on it. After a day of not knowing what to write, the Holy Spirit gently nudged, "Buy roses for the women" with a scripture attached. My earthly mindset was, "Lord, I am a missionary now. I can't go spending money like that. We are currently trying to raise an entire salary to be able to go into the mission field full-time." The kingdom mindset is to obey God and allow Him to provide. It becomes a smoother process as time goes on. I walked into a local grocery store to see if they had any deals and talked to someone about it. Nothing. I then felt drawn to go into a place called Trader Joe's. I prayed before going into the parking lot and said, "Lord, I'm believing You for provision." I found the florist and told her what I needed the roses for. After some thought, she went on saying, "Let me take you out to the back." She handed me more than fifty roses *free of charge*! Why? I have no idea. God said, "Why not? Why can't we believe for more?"

He's called, the God of the impossible, and with Jesus, *all things are possible*! I shared my story during our radical faith journey together with a subject near and dear to my heart: renewing the mind. I attached Romans 12:2 on each flower, *"Do not be conformed by the patterns of this world, but be transformed by the renewing of our minds, then you will be able to approve and test what God's will is, His good, pleasing and perfect will."* I also wrote "so loved" on each flower to remind each woman how loved they are by God. Each woman got to take a beautiful rose home provided by God.

> Which of you, if your son asks for bread,
> will give him a stone? Or if he asks for a fish, will
> give him a snake? If you, then, though you are
> evil, know how to give good gifts to your chil-

dren, how much more will your Father in heaven give good gifts to those who ask him. (Matthew 7:9–11)

Now we were nearly in August. We planned a final goodbye/fundraiser party. Our support was still not even close or near what we needed. We had a lot of one-time donations we needed for $13,000 of health coverage, for our two-year visa, and four one-way tickets. Thankfully, we already had a car in Australia that we had bought. Our conviction was to still go, even though the money wasn't there. We thought, we'd have the party, and maybe God would do a miracle there. Our friend offered, generously, to host the party at his house and cover any other needed costs, like food, tent, etc. The only day would be the day before we fly out. We agreed to it but, again, realized what a risk it was financially. Timothy and I had been contacting people about supporting us. He had a best friend from university named Jason who tragically died in a car accident after they had graduated. They both talked about becoming missionaries, and Jason, right before he died, vowed to God that he was ready to go wherever God would ask him to go. Timothy had a nudge to call Jason's parents for support. They called back the following day, and we caught up. Timothy made our need known, and they asked for another day to pray about it. We talked the next day and said they both prayed separately. The Lord spoke to both of them and told them to give us $25,000—talk about another miracle! They had a large sum of money they wanted to donate a few weeks before our phone call but didn't know who to give it to. We had not spoken to them in years, then we called, and they were obedient to a large sum of money. Both Timothy and I were in complete shock. Again, this was days before flying to Australia.

I don't know why God sometimes comes through at the eleventh hour, especially for us, but maybe it is to see where our faith is when it comes to the unseen. We knew we were supposed to go but just had not seen the provision yet but believed God above our circumstance; and faithfully, He came through yet again. Again, there were many naysayers and people telling us we are crazy. But God likes to work in extraordinary ways. We had a conviction that He would use our story to encourage others, especially those who had doubt in our situation. When we told people, they were in absolute shock. Our hearts were not saying, "See, we told you so" but instead, "Look at Jesus, see how He works and provides." God thrives in impossible situations as He is the God of the impossible. More and more am I realizing how much He is glorified in different scenarios, whether it is healing, someone giving their life to Him, provision—you name it, He can do it. The Bible has so many stories of miracles, but I believe our lives should too. Mark 16:17–18 says, "And these signs shall follow them that believe; In my name shall they cast out devils; they shall speak with new tongues; They shall take up serpents; and if they drink any deadly thing, it shall not hurt them; they shall lay hands on the sick, and they shall recover." Let there never be a Bible scripture that we glance over or take lightly. Our lives should look like this—a life full of power and miracles. This is what He desires for us.

Chapter 16

AUSTRALIA

We had our goodbye party, received a few more donations, and off to Australia we went! We flew in on a Monday morning and went directly to staff training from the airport. The first week we were there, Timothy was with the children as training was full days that week. Sometimes it is good to be busy when there is a fourteen-hour time difference. I've found that while traveling, it's best not take naps and adjust to the time as quick as possible. It is not easy to adjust in a big-time change. I've found the children adapt quicker than we do, but there is always so much grace through it! We were temporarily living with other staff as we were given a few weeks to find housing. When you are in a foreign country, it is hard to find your first place to rent because of lack of references. Also, when you are a missionary and don't have a set weekly salary, no owner will want to rent their place to you! We had to scramble getting bank statements and other paperwork while jet-lagged and in staff training. Let me remind you, YWAM members are young adults, so they probably don't enjoy living with loud children. We wanted to find a place as quickly as possible, so we were putting in applications everywhere. One of the places was a two-bed apartment with a pool, gym, hot tub, and sauna right near the beach. We applied, and the owner said yes straight away. Finally! We found an unfurnished apartment that we could call home for two years. Now all we needed was a washing machine, refrigerator, microwave, bed frames, mattresses, furniture, kitchen supplies, and anything else you need for an apartment as all we packed were clothes.

During our DTS, we found a solid local church. They were kind enough to send out an email on our behalf, saying there was a missionary family that just moved here and was in need of furnishing an apartment. The email went out on a Wednesday, and by Sunday, we were completely blessed and moved in with everything we needed! It was a complete miracle. The appliances and some tables were given to us from our missionary organization that were allocating their number of houses into one big house. Everything else we needed was given to us by different people from the church. Not only that, but we had help with the children as we moved, plus help with moving in all the furniture up to the third floor of an apartment. I don't know how God continues to do these miracles, but I find that the more we go on in this missionary lifestyle, the easier it is to trust that He will, indeed, provide all of our needs. I remember sitting on the apartment floor in complete awe and shock of how easy that move was and how God, literally, provided everything we needed. I had not stressed about it as sometimes apartments come furnished but knew in the back of my mind He would come through yet again! Within two weeks of moving to Australia, we had our own place, which was the first time in about four years. We moved in, finished staff training, and now we're about to start staffing our first group of students and start other commitments we had on our base. We were fresh with excitement, thankful, and ready for our new journey. Moving from New York to the Sunshine Coast, Australia, was a major shift in many ways, not only the weather but also the lifestyle. New York is a fast-paced, work, work, work; busy; go, go, go type of lifestyle. Sunny Coast is a laid back, get a cup of coffee, go to the beach, don't wear shoes type of lifestyle. Little did I know, that was what my body needed to recover since the stress was still lingering.

Here we were completely new to full-time ministry as a family. We now had a three-year-old and five-year-old but have a busy schedule staffing a discipleship training school. I need to add that I am the first mom to staff in years. All the other staff are young adults, mostly eighteen to twenty-five. I knew that God wanted me to staff as a mom but didn't realize how or what that was going to look like. For the first six months of school, I decided to go to class every single day, which meant Timothy had to stay home with the children. This was his first time with having this time with them and my first time so long without them. The transition didn't bode well for a family. We didn't realize that until after a few months. I had not realized my not being home every morning of every weekday would have such an impact on the them, but it did. Timothy wasn't used to it either. It was not just mornings. There was a class some evenings too, and some days would go longer than others. In addition, I had two, one-on-ones from Germany and Norway who I met with weekly. I felt completely overwhelmed as a mom working full-time. Timothy and I would fight at times. The children were acting rebelliously. There was just a lot of tension in the house.

God spoke to Timothy and told him to do a Brazil trip during that time with Randy Clark, which was great. He had an amazing time, saw a great number of salvations and miracles, and fell in love with Brazil. It was about two weeks, so it was the first time he had been apart from the children that long, but God gave us the grace and strength to manage. Also, when he was in Brazil, the Lord put something on my heart that I will never forget. It was my ninety-eight-year-old grandmother in India. She was the only grandparent that was still alive on my side of the family. I came across a YouTube video about someone having a revelation of hell, and God just strongly impressed her upon my heart. I had a crazy thought, *Why don't we go to India in December and share the gospel with her?* He put this on my heart in October. Of course, something like this seemed impossible financially. The four of us going, between flights, visas, accommodation, food, etc. would easily be over $6,000. I shared it with Timothy and just asked him to pray about it. As the month went by, the impression just became stronger, and then finally Timothy said, "Let's go!" It would be the same time as the students were on outreach. We would even be able to surprise one of the teams in New Delhi.

The outreach leader for that team was actually the same, who led our team to Uganda! I told her about us going there, and she said they would be in Delhi for a few days. I suggested the team to, perhaps, meet my cousins while they were there, and she was very open to it. Again, my whole family in India is Hindu, so I looked at it as an opportunity to show His love to my family, not to mention my dad had planned on visiting his mother in December as well, so we had the idea to surprise him. Basically, we would be able to do some ministry, visit my family, and also plan to share the gospel with my ninety-eight-year-old grandmother. I haven't been to India since we first got married ten years previous to that. We didn't know how we were going to do it financially but decided to go, with the leading of the Holy Spirit, and take a major step of faith. The teams left for outreach, and we started to pack for our trip. Now I hadn't planned any of this in terms of how I would even be able to share the gospel with my grandmother as my dad was going to be there, and he would never let me. I knew her caretakers were Hindu, and her English wasn't good at all, but neither was my Bengali. I left these factors to the Lord and just trusted that He would work out these details. It seemed a completely impossible task, but again, I knew our God is glorified the best in impossible situations, so we had to just trust Him. We were also looking forward to the epic surprise of meeting my dad there as he was coming from New York and had no idea of us meeting him! Something like this would speak louder than the gospel to him—a crazy act of love. I certainly couldn't wait to see the look on his face!

Chapter 17

INDIA

Wbought our flights and visa and planned out our trip. We flew through Singapore to Delhi to first stop to visit my cousin. We planned on spending a few days with him and having the YWAM team meet us there for lunch. We were able to talk to him and his wife about God, and they were very open. Our children were also able to reunite and connect with theirs, which was so beautiful. We actually hadn't told the team, only the leaders, that we would be there waiting for them. They were having afternoon tea in the backyard. We put on some Indian music and came out to surprise them! They were shocked and told us stories from their outreach trip, thus far. They performed gospel skits for my cousins and their friends. My cousins were in tears. My cousin also organized a beautiful dinner for the team the next day at an expensive hotel. The team was so blessed because they had not been eating food the whole time. They had a beautiful buffet for a team of twelve people, including us, and it was more than generous. The team also had a few days to refresh, rest, and recharge before moving on. Now we had a few more days with my cousins, then we flew to Kolkata (Calcutta) where my grandmother lived. We had a YWAM contact there to see if we could do some ministry in the slums as we had a couple days before my dad arrived. Now this is amazing because I have such a heart for Indian people. God did so much in my heart about redeeming the culture to Jesus. We were able to work with orphans for a few days and take some of the team members out to dinner.

Words cannot describe how special it was, but I will never forget those few days. We then went to surprise my dad. We had found out where his hotel was and asked the workers to get him from his room for us. All of our hearts were racing. He was about the have the surprise of his life. We yelled "*surprise*" as he walked in the foyer, and he almost broken down. My children ran up to him and gave him a huge hug. I could just see the shock and love in his eyes. It was one of the most beautiful memories of my life and the most epic surprise my dad had ever experienced! We reconnected later in the day and made plans to go and see his mother. This was such a sweet moment as there were three generations of Dutta (my maiden name) all in one room. My grandmother, we call her Thama, was more than thrilled to see us and our children. It was a truly serene moment with tears filling the entire room. It has always been so hard to have all of my family in India because I never grew up around my grandparents, aunts, uncles, and cousins. So the few times we went there, we cherish and prize every moment we had time with our family. It's surreal when my three-year-old daughter, Priya, got to meet her ninety-eight-year-old grandmother. There are no words to describe our first visit, but they weren't even needed. There was enough body language and love to write a book. My grandmother only knows a couple words in English, but again, the love and expression on her face was so powerful. Her servants were grateful, too, that we came to visit as, normally, she didn't have many visitors. We planned visiting her again the next day.

We waited to meet our dad, but he didn't show up at the meeting spot. We then went to his hotel to see what was going on. He was completely bedridden and sick from some kind of food poisoning. We were really concerned but knew he would be okay. We thought, *Do we go and see my grandmother without him?* Yes! This was our opportunity to share the gospel with her! We remembered the language barrier, so we contacted our YWAM friends there to see if they would be willing to translate. They said yes right away. We organized a time and realized this moment would be precious. Her answer to the gospel would dictate where she would spend eternity.

With my heart racing, we met our friends (translators) and headed over to my grandmother's. Our friend, who is a worshipper, came with us. I had no idea what to expect but knew God was up to something as He was the one Who put this crazy thought into my head months back. The servants welcomed us at the door and were excited to have us. As usual, my grandmother's face lit up when she saw us and our children. We were aware we had a short window of time to share the most important message in the world. Again, I wasn't sure how we were going to share with the Hindu servants there. A few minutes after arriving, they offered us tea. Now this isn't like America where you grab a Lipton tea bag and add sugar and milk. They make it with fresh spices in a pot full of fresh milk, and it takes time. Our translators looked at us and said, "Yes, take the tea!" We knew this would be our window of opportunity to share the message with her. So basically, the three factors that I had originally thought would be hindrances all suddenly disappeared. My dad got sick, so he couldn't make it, God brought us translators, and now the servants would leave the room for about twenty minutes to make fresh Indian chai tea.

I sat down next to her with the translator and, in faith, started to share the gospel. I spoke slowly from the heart and tried to make it as simple as possible. I could tell she was very open and even looked excited. We shared with her that Jesus heals and could heal the Alzheimer's that she had and her memory. At the end, we explained to her that if she wanted, she could say yes to God and be in heaven eternally. We paused, and she completely wanted to accept Jesus into her heart. To make the story even more amazing, at the end, she said, "Now I am a child of God!" I did not even explain this part to her when I shared the gospel with her. And to make it even crazier, she said it in English! I believe she said that as confirmation for us to say she understood everything that we had said. Was it really that easy and effortless? Yes. God put it on hearts to do, we obeyed, and He opened the door because He knew she was ready. Now someone else in my family had said "yes" to Jesus at ninety-eight years of age!

It was a complete miracle. We had our worshipper friend sing a few songs, and she was moved to tears. I saw an incredible joy on her face and realized I had witnessed one of the most amazing miracles of my life. God does leave the ninety-nine to go after the one. He sent us from Australia to Kolkata to share the gospel with "the one." Did we do other things while we were there? Of course. But we went to India with one focus, and it was her. I will never forget that day, how simple it was, and the fact that I now know she will spend eternity in heaven. Nothing is better than that!

We visited another part of India to see more family and then flew back to Australia. Our two-week trip was nothing short of special. God calls us to share the gospel wherever we go for big crowds or for the person sitting across from us. The question is, will we be obedient to the tugging of His Spirit when He speaks? It could be a stranger on the street or a family member. He could prompt us to fly to another part of the world or share the gospel with someone at work. I believe the more times we say yes to God and not quench the Spirit, the more He will move through us on His behalf. It is all about trusting Him. I could have easily told God that we didn't have the finances (we didn't), reminded Him of all the factors, and could have made a lot more excuses of why not to go, but I didn't. He builds our faith in situations like this; and if we had the answers, resources, and understanding to every situation, then why would we need faith? Faith is in the unseen, not the seen. Hebrews 11:1 says, "Now faith is confidence in what we hope for and assurance about what we do not see."

We flew back to Australia and celebrated Christmas. It was quite odd going from celebrating Christmas in the cold and snow for our whole life to hot and humid Australia where people have barbecues on the beach. We received a phone call from our parents, and my mom was in shock, saying, "Jonali! Thamma (my dad's mom) has her memory back!" She has been remembering things! Also, she has been able to eat by herself and go to the bathroom alone! Now, we hadn't told my parents anything, so they didn't understand what had happened and didn't know we prayed for her. When a ninety-eight-year-old with Alzheimer's suddenly starts remembering things, it is an absolute miracle. Timothy and I were shocked, but we weren't because we prayed and believed. My parents were completely dumbfounded. After we got off the phone with them, we wanted to be wise with what we told them. We had video of us praying with her, so we put it on YouTube and sent the private link to my parents. We called my parents and asked them to watch the video. They were surprised and still had doubt in their hearts, but I believe there was some belief since it was one of the first miracles they had seen with their own eyes. Even believers don't see miracles like that, so for my Hindu parents to witness their almost one-hundred-year-old, mom have a complete shift, it is hard to deny that God exists.

Chapter 18

Marriage and Ministry

In life, there are highs, and there are lows as well. In our first almost six months in ministry, we became aware that our marriage and parenting needed some serious attention. We decided to step down from ministry to focus on life on the home front. We sought counseling for a part of that time as well. I spent time with the Lord in this pit of worthlessness and saw a picture of Jesus giving me a gorgeous huge, clear, spotless diamond. He said to me, "You are valuable, Jonali." He then confirmed it with the scripture that says in Proverbs 31:10: "A wife of noble character who can find? She is worth far more than rubies." Not only did He speak the truth about my value in Him louder than the lie, but He gave me a picture too. I believe God speaks like this a lot. I believe, the more we spend time with Him, the more detailed we can get pictures, dreams, and visions. In one sentence, He healed trauma and lies of my past. We just need to allow the truth to be much louder than the lie, no matter what it seems like! The woman who was counseling me was incorporating Jesus into everything. We would pray, and she would let the Holy Spirit speak directly through me. One picture I saw was Jesus holding a bowl and out of the faucet came snakes. I was surprised by this picture until He gave me more detail and said that the snakes coming out of the faucet represented lies and deception I had believed for most of my life. I then immediately saw Jesus smashing them to the ground in one second. That was parallel to the death on the cross and what He did for our sin.

Why in the world do we still believe lies when He died so we could have life and life abundant. The enemy loves to distract with death. I remember her reading Psalm 91 over me where God was talking to me about being safe in Him. He showed me a picture of the gross matter that comes out after giving birth. I saw Jesus dumping it into the wilderness. He asked me, "Why would you go back into the wilderness to seek out the things that need to be disposed of and was seen no more?" He said, "I took care of it on the cross. You are a new creation." Will a baby ever see any of that? Of course not. It's gone, and the baby is new! Jesus was also putting His hand on my back, reminding me that He loves me and is with me. Although Jesus makes so many amazing promises in His word, there is nothing like when He speaks to you directly. Like I said before, sometimes one line directly from God can heal years of lies that the enemy has thrown. He spoke worth into my worthlessness.

Although there are many scriptures about our value in Christ, nothing beats the Father's voice directly as it hits the heart loud and clear! He spoke strongly to me on Ezekiel 47 about the river from the temple. I will put the whole passage in here because it is so important to understand it as a whole. Here are verses 1 to 12:

> The man brought me back to the entrance to the temple, and I saw water coming out from under the threshold of the temple toward the east (for the temple faced east). The water was coming down from under the south side of the temple, south of the altar. The man brought me back to the entrance to the temple, and I saw water coming out from under the threshold of the temple toward the east (for the temple faced east). The water was coming down from under the south side of the temple, south of the altar. He then brought me out through the north gate and led me around the outside to the outer gate facing

east, and the water was trickling from the south side. As the man went eastward with a measuring line in his hand, he measured off a thousand cubits and then led me through water that was ankle-deep. He measured off another thousand cubits and led me through water that was knee-deep. He measured off another thousand and led me through water that was up to the waist. He measured off another thousand, but now it was a river that I could not cross, because the water had risen and was deep enough to swim in—a river that no one could cross. He asked me, "Son of man, do you see this?" Then he led me back to the bank of the river. When I arrived there, I saw a great number of trees on each side of the river. He said to me, "This water flows toward the eastern region and goes down into the Arabah, where it enters the Dead Sea. When it empties into the sea, the salty water there becomes fresh. Swarms of living creatures will live wherever the river flows. There will be large numbers of fish, because this water flows there and makes the salt water fresh; so where the river flows everything will live. Fishermen will stand along the shore; from En Gedi to En Eglaim there will be places for spreading nets. The fish will be of many kinds—like the fish of the Mediterranean Sea. But the swamps and marshes will not become fresh; they will be left for salt. Fruit trees of all kinds will grow on both banks of the river. Their leaves will not wither, nor will their fruit fail. Every month they will bear fruit, because the water from the sanctuary flows to them. Their fruit will serve for food and their leaves for healing.

Holy Spirit immediately said to me, "Do you want ankle-deep or knee-deep faith, or do you want to go swimming in a river where My life can flow? If you flow in Me, all this fruit can come out of your life, and anything you touch will have life and fruit attached to it." I was stunned. I have been a believer for almost twenty years but have found myself going back and forth from being fully committed to complacency. Are we living for a Jesus-on-the-side gospel, or are we willing to really lay down our life for Him daily? A Christian brother, named Ravi Kendall, had a word for me once when he was praying for me, saying, "No one should have gone through what you did." He had a word of knowledge. I bring this up to say that this was why I kept going back and forth between fully committed and complacent because I couldn't let my past go. So much of my past dictated what I believed as it was eighteen years of my life. My past spoke louder than the truth. The lies were louder than the truth. Those eighteen years (or centuries of traditions/generational bloodlines) of familiar spirits lingered until I was ready and willing to believe Jesus over the circumstance. It takes a complete brain rewire! Lies are an utter deception and illusion from the enemy! I would like to share a conversation I had with the Lord in the midst of pain and brokenness just to simply show that He speaks, and how we know its Him:

"Did my past break your heart?"

"I wept, Jonali."

"Will you be gentle in the healing process?"

"I won't even break a bruised reed."

"What about fasting?"

"Do your best, I'll bless it."

"What about ministry?

"Me, Jonali, give your dreams to Me."

"What about years of strongholds in my mind?"

"Too easy for Me."

"Why am I still struggling?"

"Your eyes are still fixed on problems."

"What should I do?"

"My thoughts are higher. My ways are better."

"Is freedom far?"

"It seems so far. It's already there, Jonali. Walk in it." (Galatians 5:1)

"Why can't transformation be overnight?"

"It's a choice, and relationship is two-way."

"Is there a set time for healing?"

"It's your heart, Jonali."

"How do I focus on You?"

"Fall in love."

"Anything else?"

"Obedience unlocks freedom more than anything. My strength is made perfect in your weakness. All you have to do is obey."

"Why do I have such a hard time?"

"Fear of getting hurt by Me and Timothy. Trust Me with your heart and Timothy with your heart."

"Have I ever let you down in the past?"

"No," He sighed. "Every time there is a choice to take "safe" route, you take it, but it's hindering you from all that I have for you."

He reminds me about a song where there's a lyric that goes: "And further and further, my heart moves away from the shore. Whatever it looks like, whatever may come, I am Yours," meaning, safety is away from the shore. It's in the unseen places of the deep.

He ended the conversation like this: "Freedom doesn't just fall into your lap, it comes with faith, trust, and surrender. What will you choose today? The cage or the sky? Go and fly, Jonali."

Right after having this deep conversation with God, and I had a conversation with someone that challenged and asked me, "Do you expect God for the best?"

I said, "No, I struggle with doubt and unbelief in that area of my life. Our refrigerator broke down, and we asked our church to send an email to see if anyone had an old one."

Someone from the church called us the day after, saying that they wanted to buy us a new one. We could hardly believe it! God spoke loudly, saying that He was into making things new, not repairing the old. This blessing spoke loudly to what He was doing spiritually in my life. I was so grateful. Never did I think, as a missionary, that we would own a nicer fridge than we did when we were making great money in New York on two salaries. It was the nicest refrigerator we've ever had as it was a more expensive, stainless steel one. My old mindset was to get a used one. We are missionaries. We can get by, but sometimes God likes to speak and bless loudly through our circumstances, and this beautiful couple heard from God to bless us in this way! He furnished our entire apartment in Australia. How could I not believe Him for a fridge? He whispered to me, "I didn't want you to settle for an old one but to be blessed by a new one as a picture to show you that I have great things in store for you." He then dropped 1 Corinthians 2:9 in my heart: "However, as it is written: 'What no eye has seen, what no ear has heard, and what no human mind has conceived'—the things God has prepared for those who love him." He reminded me to not glance over these biblical words but to soak them into my heart and meditate on them.

Stress came because we didn't know how to balance family and ministry well, so our marriage became stagnant, and our kids were really acting up and rebelling, feeling like they were not a priority in our lives. We had the amazing support of our base leaders and our church. They helped us through these trials. We really needed a lot of healing as there were some deep wounds. Timothy and I began to talk about areas in our marriage that needed help. We also sought some counseling for a time where we would meet with a couple separately and then together again. This was the first time in ten years that we had done this, and it was really helpful. We each had separate wounds from our past that needed some salve and balm on. It was a very humbling yet a very needed time. We also had a chat with our three- and five-year-old and apologized for allowing them to feel second to ministry. I realized the quick shift of motherhood full-time to only part-time was too quick for them and the same to my husband for throwing him into full-time dad role for a few months. Childcare was just too expensive, so we really had to take care of them ourselves. We saw them sometimes, as a hindrance, instead of embracing the messiness of taking them with us.

In YWAM, being more of a young adult ministry, there hadn't any families staffing the DTS with us. I was the only mom on staff where everyone else was under twenty-five. I didn't understand at twenty-five what it was like having children, let alone having them in ministry. We were so thankful we took a few months off to allow the Holy Spirit to teach us the perfect harmony of family and ministry. If we had kept going and ignored the immediate needs at home, the wounds would have only festered and grown. It would have been a downward spiral that would have eventually just blown up. But God knew we needed a drastic change and to have the support around us we needed to thrive and grow. God spoke loudly about the bitterness in my heart. I thought it was protecting me from being hurt again, but it was false. It was sin. It was an illusion.

And it kept me from being free. I had allowed roots of bitterness to go deep and, not being submissive for a long time, to become a habit. God can loosen the soil and uproot, but we need to obey, allow, and yield. It is not our right anymore as Christians. We died so that He could live. We build walls thinking they are protecting us, yet they were actually keeping us from experiencing the abundant life that He has. Unfortunately, it is usually the people close to us where we have bitterness in our hearts—whether a spouse, parent, close friends, people in ministry, or work. Isn't that the enemy's tactic? And we walk around proclaiming to be Christians, yet we are not continually forgiving the people closest to us—seventy-seven times seven, right? A whole decade of marriage, I had so much bitterness in my heart toward my spouse. I would sulk in my bedroom countless times after fighting. I remember my body feeling the bitterness, physically, by having chest pain and sometimes body weakness because I had internalized it. Because of my sensitivity to words, you can guess what the enemy used the most to attack our marriage—words. I would go over them in my mind again and again. I call that dwelling on sin, an imaginary cloud of bitterness that God needed to burst. I would argue everything. I would see decisions he made as a way to control me instead of protecting me. If there wasn't submission toward my husband, there definitely was not to God and, out of that, rebellion, which is the spirit of witchcraft. I believe there is a tie here to rejection, and if we don't sort it out with the Lord, it can lead to affairs or promiscuity. One of the lies I believed was that I was too deep in bitterness to change and that I was already in my mid-thirties and couldn't change. If I allowed that lie to fester, it could have been like the story of Jacob and where Esau sold his birthright for a temporary piece of meat. Satan goes for our weakness at an opportune time.

I recall a story once of someone having a dream to start a soccer club in a third-world country. He wanted to have a space where kids could learn soccer for free. Well, that grew and began competing with the larger premier leagues. Soon he was flying first class, rubbing shoulders with big names. His marriage, however, was falling apart. Their child was struggling at home. He was a visionary but did not have the character to match the calling. The family split, and he stepped down from the dream he once had. I want to share this example, not as pointing any fingers, but with pure humility, in saying, that could have been me. How many times have we heard stories of pastors cheating on their wives, ministry children falling away from the Lord, or ministries falling apart out of nowhere? I don't believe they fall apart out of nowhere but instead as a lack of building a strong foundation in Him and letting God refine our character. Timothy and I were desperate to rebuild a foundation that was full of cracks. We wanted to do, whatever it took for us, to get on a smooth track once again. If we ignore the root of the problem, this can be a great danger and hindrance to what God has for us.

First Timothy 3 is an instruction for overseers and deacons. Here is what it says, starting in verse 2:

> Now the overseer is to be above reproach, faithful to his wife, temperate, self-controlled, respectable, hospitable, able to teach, not given to drunkenness, not violent but gentle, not quarrelsome, not a lover of money. He must manage his own family well and see that his children obey him and he must do so in a manner worthy of full respect. (If anyone does not know how to manage his own family, how can he take care of God's church). He must not be a recent convert, or he may become conceited and fall under the same judgement as the devil. He must also have a good

> reputation with outsiders, so that he will not fall into disgrace and into the devil's trap. In the same way, deacons are to be worth of respect, sincere, not indulging in much wine, and not pursuing dishonest gain. They must keep hold of the deep truths of faith with a clear conscience. They must first be tested; and then if there is nothing against them, let them serve as deacons. In the same way, the women are to be worthy of respect, not malicious talkers but temperate and trustworthy in everything. A deacon must be faithful to his wife and must manage his children and his household well. Those who have served well gain and excellent standing and great assurance in their faith in Christ Jesus. (verse 13)

I don't know about you, but that sounds a very high standard. If anyone were to look in the mirror and ask themselves if they represent that scripture well, they would feel intimidated.

Timothy and I have had years of "character refinement." Over the past few years, we see this as something of utmost importance. We have a strong conviction that, if things are disarray at home, we need to take a step back and reaccess ministry. We cannot live as hypocrites and be fighting at home. The kids are out of control yet preach from a pulpit and look amazing just because we have a gift of charisma. Words lack power if you don't practice what you preach. I have learned over the years that I can learn from and respect people a lot more if I know what their personal life looks like when they are at home. I've met and listened to too many people that know scripture but don't know their Father who wrote it. I remember once the Holy Spirit saying, "Jonali, if I were to put a camera in your home and play it, would you look the same as you are when you're doing ministry?" A deep conviction overwhelmed me because of the way I had been talking to my husband and kids. But when I was around people who I was doing ministry with, my tone and words looked rather different. The last thing I wanted was to be two Jonalis. One person at home and a completely different person in the public. I immediately repented, and asked God to change me from the inside, out. I yearned to have the same character in whatever role I was in—mother, wife, friend, or mentor. I now have a strong conviction to never teach or preach anything that I am not living myself. If that means I don't have a pulpit for a while, I am completely content with that. I've learned that the state of our heart is so much more than what our hearts appear to be to other people. Our words can carry much more power if we actually believe and live what we say.

I am so thankful that God has taught us so much in the first few years of ministry. We cannot afford to have any cracks. You don't want to build a home and it is only half done then completely collapses because the foundation wasn't right or the winds came and blew it down.

> Therefore everyone who hears these words of mine and puts them into practice is like a wise man who built his house on the rock. The rain came down, the streams rose, and the winds blew and beat against that house; yet it did not fall, because it had its foundation on the rock. But everyone who hears these words of mine and does not put them into practice is like a foolish man who built his house on sand. The rain came down, the streams rose, and the winds blew and beat against that house, and it fell with a great crash. (Matthew 7:24–27)

Jesus talks about actually living out what the Bible says here. If we live what the Bible says, our foundation will be rock solid. And when trials will come, nothing will make the house crumble because it was built on a firm foundation. However, if we read the Bible but don't obey what it says, then we are in danger of our house crashing. It doesn't say the house just fell, but it fell with a great crash. It continues and ends in verse 28: "When Jesus had finished saying these things, the crowds were amazed at his teaching, because he taught as one who had authority, and not as their teachers of the law." You teach with authority when you live what you preach. I believe the Holy Spirit gives people discernment to make them aware, especially if they don't know you personally or whether you live what you preach or not. It's interesting how it also distinguishes Jesus from the teachers of the law. I'm sure it is referring to teachers who might not have been living what they were preaching. For example, the teachers of the law, or Pharisees, were always busy pointing out the speck in someone's eye and not seeing the plank in their own.

There have been many times in my life where I have ignored the Holy Spirit for a long period of time, so I have experienced those great crashes, whether it was dating a nonbeliever for a year, ignoring sin in my life, or almost losing my life. I am completely guilty of not obeying God at certain times in my life. I can say, however, with 100 percent confidence that you never win when you ignore God or when you have seared your conscience to the extreme of not feeling remorse over sin. Hearts harden when we remain in unrepentant sin. The Bible says in 1 Timothy 4:2 that some will abandon the faith and describe their conscience as "being seared with a hot iron." It's like getting burned so many times with a hot iron that it doesn't even feel hot anymore. That is what it is like for people who ignore their sin over and over again and continue to indulge in it. It also says in Ephesians 4:18–19, "Because of the hardness of their heart (have) become callous." It is saying, we can't live any longer like the gentiles do as "they are darkened in their understanding and separated from the life of God because of the ignorance that is in them due to the hardening of their hearts. Having lost all sensitivity, they have given themselves over to sensuality so as to indulge in every kind of impurity." I am sure we can name many people in our lives like that, but what if we learned how to be introspective and look at the state of our own hearts? There are seasons where I get on my knees before God and ask Him what areas in my life has my heart become calloused or hardened. If He shows me, I will repent and turn away and apologize to anyone that I need to. We can't just "starve" the sin in our life, or it will come back or revisit itself at some point. I've had to fill the gap with His personal words and His word over me so I can truly be free in an area. Galatians 5:1 says, "It is for freedom that Christ has set us free. Stand firm, then, and do not let yourselves be burdened again by a yoke of slavery." Satan's tactic is to keep us in our sin. But how can we stay in slavery if Christ died to set us completely free at the cross?

I personally think that if we stay in this posture before God, He will honor that as He is always concerned the most with the state of our heart. What if we asked Him, not even every few weeks but every few days, if we did something where we need to repent? I believe, if we obey, it will keep our heart posture soft and open before Go. Then there will be nothing to block our relationship with Him.

Many times, it is easy to cover heart sin, whether you are in ministry or not. The scary part is when ministry leaders cover it up. Maybe they fear, if they tell someone, they will be asked to step down from their position, or they will be embarrassed about what people think of them. The key is to always remain humble. There are so many scriptures in the Bible, especially in proverbs, about taking correction. If you have pride, correction definitely won't be something you are seeking out. Now if you're anything like me, I don't bat my eyelashes when my husband corrects me on something. Usually, I have a heart attitude of "Here we go again," or "What about ___ in your life?" It is because I know that he is right. I had to learn that it is always out of love. Hebrews 12:6 says, "Because the Lord disciplines the one he loves, and he chastens everyone he accepts as his son." He basically says the same thing in Proverbs 3:12.

Timothy doesn't correct me because he doesn't love me. But because he loves me, he corrects me. He wants better for me. His heart's motive and intention are good, and as long as he's doing it with the right heart and motive, it is my job to be able to receive it, learn from it, and grow. We have been married for twelve years and believe I take it better now than I did before. All I had to do was make the switch in my brain that it was coming from love, not spite. It was coming from a place of him wanting what is best for me. He wants to see me living in the fullness of Christ. Hebrews 12:9–11 says, "Moreover, we have all had human fathers who disciplined us and we respected them for it. How much more should we submit to the Father of our spirits and live! Our Fathers disciplined us for a little while as they thought best; but God disciplines us for our good, that we may share in his holiness. No discipline seems pleasant at the time, but painful. Later on, however, it produces a harvest of righteousness and peace for those who have been trained by it." It talks, yet again here, about submitting to God. It also says, He disciplines us for our good. It goes on to explain that it is never pleasant at the time but indeed hurts. The good news is the last part where it says that it "produces a harvest of righteousness and peace for those trained by it." So if we don't listen and we rebel, we will not have the peace that follows the training. It's for our good! I believe that it all boils down to correcting our thinking in *Who* is disciplining us and what is their heart behind it. Timothy and I, of course, discipline our children. It isn't because we hate them but because we love them and desire to see them grow and learn from their mistakes. It actually is not hurting them but helping them. The greater lesson is obeying their parents, which will indeed create a "harvest of righteousness" for their future!

Chapter 19

CHILDREN AND MINISTRY

Something we decided to pick up in this season was homeschooling. I had never planned on homeschooling our children. It was never on my radar, nor could I ever see myself doing it. I have the degrees to teach French, and did so for three years, but never thought about teaching my own. Now that Elijah was five, I had to start thinking about schooling for him. Although there were a few Christian schools locally that were good, Timothy and I both felt to begin homeschooling. We weren't sure why, but we obeyed. We do know that it went along with our desire to have our children to be part of ministry. We also loved the flexibility that if God spoke and said to spontaneously do a mission's trip, we weren't bound to the school calendar. Priya was still only three, so I didn't feel rushed to start anything with her, although her brother had been through preschool. Thankfully, my son picked up his alphabet and reading quickly. I chose a curriculum that was independent so that once he started reading and writing, he could learn independently. With his type A personality, this worked out well. I only needed a couple hours with him every morning. We have been doing family devotionals every morning before anything else, and then I school them. And by lunchtime, they are free. Homeschooling was completely new to me, but God gave me the grace to somehow learn how to do it.

Motherhood is definitely challenging. I've come to know, and always tell people, you don't realize how dead you are to yourself until you have children. They become your everything, and so often, it is hard to see the blood, sweat, and tears that go into this role, much of adulthood ministry looks like, helping to repair and heal wounds from childhood. This, automatically, gives more of a fear of the Lord in mothering because I would never want my words or actions to taint how they view the world later in their life. I realize how important words were to me, growing up as a child, and how I have to consciously think about what I say or how to talk to them. I find myself continually apologizing for not using the right tone or expecting too much out of them for their age. Being a mom can bring out your best and your worst. The beautiful part about it is that, with God, we can transform for the better for our children. There have been times in my life where I looked at them as if they were a burden or as, I mentioned, to put ministry before them, but I have always taken this back to the cross, and God has been able to expose so much in my heart. It's never easy when God prunes, but its only to bear more fruit. In the days of the baby/toddler stages of life where it was physically draining, you can't seem to see the fruit of your labor—changing diapers, making sandwiches, and feeling you aren't getting anything done all day. The problem is, this is a beautiful stage because you are laboring for God. And although the kids might not be old enough to notice what you do for them, it can be so rewarding when they smile when you pick them up or when you watch them fall asleep in your arms. These are the memories we never forget and wish we could either freeze time or go back to when they were younger.

Although the kids are still young, I've been able to stay at home with them full-time or be in ministry full-time with them. I would say, I have been completely satisfied in both and know that if God asked me to take a season off to focus on them only, I would. They are my ministry. They are more important than any platform, book, or ministry opportunity. I remember a woman, named Lisa Bevere, turned down an invitation to be the keynote speaker at a Hillsong women's conference in Australia because it was her children's vacation, and she wanted to spend time with them instead of speaking. I believe that is admirable to turn down an invitation to one of the most influential churches in the world today for the sake of your children. It would probably be a dream of mine to speak at a conference like that as I have a heart for women and, specifically, renewing the mind. I would hope to be able to do the same thing if the timing wasn't right. Life is all about choices, and our choice, big or small, have a large effect on those around us. As a mom, it is important that our children know they are important to us. I have spent too much time on a mobile phone or on a laptop when I should be spending more face-to-face time with them. I understand, if you're a working mom and have to do what you have to do, but I believe if we are able, our time can really be guarded for them. Their behavior can be a direct sign of parenting. When our children misbehave more, it's because they aren't getting the attention or discipline they need at home. We have to be intentional with them until they are eighteen so that we set them up for victory once they leave the home.

> Train up a child in the way he should go;
> and when he is old, he will not depart from it.
> (Proverbs 22:6)

We can't take these crucial years back. With God, we have the strength to be the best parents we were made to be for our children. Sometimes it means reading that extra book to them or doing that craft or stepping away from our busy schedules, periodically, to make a lifelong investment. It's all about sowing and reaping. Galatians 6:7 says, "Do not be deceived, God is not mocked; for whatever a man sows, that he will also reap." We need to ask ourselves regularly: What are we sowing into our children? Are we speaking words of life or death? Are we being too hard with them? Are we challenging them and giving them room to grow? Some of my biggest heroes in life are the homeschooling mothers of six, seven, or eight children that I have met. They have given up their life for them and are the most giving people I know. They rarely carry stress or anxiety but have a peace where they solely depend on God for their strength. It challenges me when I am around them as I currently have two children and show more stress than them! They carry one of the most beautiful life lessons: being completely dead to yourself. Their children love each other well and spread chores out so beautifully. These are some of the most beautiful, well-behaved children I have ever met, and it all goes to those no-named mothers who will never have a platform, but they are warriors for God, and their children tend to follow the Lord as they grow older. I see their character and am completely inspired. They are absolute servants and mentors. They could write books about their journeys but are probably too busy investing in their children. We should bless mothers always. Whether it is—buying them a coffee or to tell a tired mom whose kids are out of control in a store that they are doing a great job or giving them a gift card to buy something for themselves. Moms are often overlooked yet are some of the strongest people I know. Whether it's the single mother raising her children because her husband left her or the working mom who needs to hire an au pair/nanny for a reason or the stay-at-home mom where her husband travels on a regular basis, we all have different circumstances. But with God, we are able to get through any trial. Again, it's a mindset of surrendering because that is where the strength and power comes from. It never comes from ourselves because this is when burnout occurs. I often need to take a time-out to pray so a week doesn't go by and feel like I'm at my end. We need to continually drink the water that we have free and never-ending access to spiritually so that we never run dry!

It doesn't matter if the schools we send our children to are Christian or not. They don't have to be Christian to go to a Christian school. Most of the time, private schools just want the money. Parents will send their child to a Christian school that have teachers who follow God and not teach evolution. However, a child seems to be more influenced by its peers. First Corinthians 15:33 says, "Do not be misled, Bad company corrupts good character." It doesn't matter if you are a child or an adult; this scripture applies. We need to surround ourselves with like-minded people who will challenge us and bring us closer to the Lord. If a child is strong enough in their faith to influence the friend they have and not be influenced, then I believe it's okay to keep that friendship. But if we see our child being negatively influenced by another, we will recognize they aren't ready yet. Mine are only five and seven, so they are still very young. Will they go to public school one day? Possibly, but only if Timothy and I know they are influencers, not allowing people to influence them. I remember at a local library here in Australia, they were doing a story time for children under five. They had a person dressed as a witch telling scary stories. When I was young, nothing of that kind would ever be possible! We've had to talk to parents (who we are friends with) about how we had seen their children treat ours. These are hard conversations, and for someone like me who hates confrontation, it really tests the people-pleasing spirit. Our role as parents is to be protectors of our kids, and if it requires hard conversations with our friends that may risk losing a friendship, it has to be worth it for the sake of our children at their vulnerable, impressionable age.

We were created to be the perfect parents for our children, and how we mother or father during their childhood will have an enormous impact on who they turn into as an adult. I don't care what profession my children end up having. But what I do care about is their character and how they treat and love people. For me, good character is the most important thing to see in our children. And as they are young, we teach them to put others first and love people well. Are they perfect at this all the time? Of course not. But we pray and ask God that they will know Him personally so that, as they receive God's love, it will be natural to pour onto others. I believe this is the most important jobs as parents as we are a walking testimony to the goodness of God every day of our lives. If we live one way but talk a different way, they will see the hypocrisy, and we risk them wanting nothing to do with God as they grow older. If we live in a way that exemplifies the fruit of the spirit but also the miraculous and genuine love, I believe, with all my heart, they will want the same.

I've been in ministry for, well, over a decade now and have seen too many children who grow up where their parents were too busy to realize what was actually going on at home—a child getting raped by a family member or missionary children who are left with the locals and are raped by pastors, kids that are suicidal and want nothing to do with God. This is not okay. We need to be aware of who our child is left with. All it takes is one instance of evil to scar a child for the rest of their life. I always ask the same question when I hear horror stories like this: Where were the parents? What were they doing? Were they spiritually blind to not know what was happening to their own flesh and blood, or were they too busy ministering or working, not to see what was going on with their own children? As parents, we have a real responsibility to know who we leave our children with. I don't want to speak any condemnation over anyone where it was a situation out of their control or where they really trusted someone and feel the guilt from it now. God has the ability to heal and forgive anyone and any situation.

I challenge those whose children now are young. Don't be afraid to seriously look into different daycare situations. Or if you get a bad feeling about a babysitter, it's not worth it. As parents, we have 100 percent responsibility over our children. I believe this includes what they watch on TV or iPad. We don't allow ours to watch anything with witches, fairytales, magic, etc. Coming from Hinduism, I am a lot more sensitive to the spiritual realm and don't want them being exposed to anything demonic. I grew up with Hindu gods, statues, and idols around my house. Timothy and I had such a strong conviction once on burning anything in our home that could have negative influence on our household. An example is getting souvenirs from overseas. We threw a statue down on the driveway and ashes coming out. We both had weird pains in our bodies when we smashed and burned things. But this "spiritual housecleaning" had side effects, so to speak, and it was our conviction at the time to get anything out of the house that could have negative spiritual effects on our house. Some people would think we are extreme or legalistic, but it was our conviction at the time. Whether it's a TV show, a game, supporting a restaurant or author, everyone has different convictions and have to live by them.

God asked me to give up coffee. I would never say to someone that drinking coffee is a sin, but it was a personal conviction to me for a season. With the new age really coming out, we need to monitor what gets infiltrated into libraries and schools. I have heard before that the new age movement that is coming out is basically repackaged Hinduism. Again, coming from Hinduism, I can totally see why. Superstition is huge in Hinduism and the new age movement. Believing you're doing something for good luck or to gain inner peace is believing a huge lie. There is no peace without Jesus Christ. I'm most at peace when I am talking to Him or when He's talking to me, when my heart is pure, and I've repented of anything that can be sin in my life. Emptying your mind or using herbs to gain peace is not biblical. Rest comes from relationship. A lot of these practices seemed more geared toward women, too, as many of them have strong marketing angles. Sometimes, women can be led more by their emotions, which is why these parties are geared toward them. The products can be used to create a distraction, too, because of going to them before going God.

Why can't we have more home groups or times of getting into the presence of God together? This is the best medicine we can go to. I was healed of a disease because Jesus was my doctor. He told me exactly what to do, and I got better, which answers the question of why He said so loudly, "I am the answer." He was the answer, and He gave me the prescription I needed to be healed, which was to renew my mind and my thought process. If I skipped this and just took medicine and followed the earthly doctor, I believe I would have still been sick today. God spoke loudly and told me to throw away the medications. I am so glad I trusted Him as it was a huge faith step. Because the new age has a lot of ties to Hinduism, I've seen so many of my Christian friends dabble in things that appear harmless, but they don't see it and are therefore opening doors for the enemy to come in. This is for another book, but we really need to be careful of what we expose ourselves to and what we open our bodies up to. If we need to go to anything or anyone but Jesus for peace, health, or relaxation, then we need to question if we really believe what the Bible says. It doesn't matter if the most respected Christian leader is doing it. There isn't room for compromise.

A lot of these movements have a correlation with positive thinking. We can "positively think" ourselves out of believing we need Jesus. We are to think on scripture and truth. If God is the giver of life and satisfies every living thing, then why is it, in the body of Christ, we are always searching for new things to find peace or purpose in life? I think it's worse when money is involved, and we find ourselves in pyramid schemes, and our motives become twisted. I've seen many women sell products through the church and host parties where friendships become based on sales. Once I was invited to one of these parties, and I told the girl that I had a conviction against what she was selling and remember the look on her face was mortified. Sometimes it seems, relationships can be based on "what can you do for me," especially when it comes to ministry and the church. Favoritism sneaks into the church so easily. And although it is completely unbiblical, it can become rampant. Leaders in ministry tend to get favored where others get overlooked. There have been many times when Timothy and I have said no to opportunities because we knew that they weren't God as we aren't necessarily, "yes, men." We've let down many leaders in life and found that we have been treated differently because of it. At the end of the day, we need to follow our conviction.

After about six months, we felt the release to step back into ministry. Our YWAM base felt called to start weekly evangelism, and I staffed DTS once again. Timothy and I went over the schedule together and worked out a good balance of family and ministry. This time, my commitment was a lot less. Instead of going to class every day during the week, I went only twice. I also had a couple of one-on-ones that I would meet with weekly. We also decided to have a couple of meals with the students in the evenings and brought our children with us. We took them on coffee dates and worked better to keep them a part of everything, instead of separating them for ministry. Would I be able to do this with a baby and toddler? Probably not. I stayed at home with them when they were young, and Timothy worked full-time. Priya was still only three, so of course, it wasn't orderly all the time with life interruptions. I learned to embrace them and not to get annoyed or frustrated. I came to the realization that "kids will be kids" and won't be perfect all the time. They would interrupt in class, and we had to break up their fighting at coffee shops. Would people get annoyed sometimes? Yes. We had to elevate the importance of doing ministry as a family over people-pleasing.

Jesus knows the importance of children. We get a glimpse of that in one of the gospels: "Then people brought little children to Jesus for him to place his hands on them and pray for them. But the disciples rebuked them Jesus said, 'Let the little children come to me, and do not hinder them, for the kingdom of heaven belongs to such as these.' When he had placed his hands on them, he went on from there" (Matthew 19:13–15). We tried to be creative and have "coffee date only" toys so they were special and wouldn't get bored with them. We also rewarded them when they behaved and got disciplined when they didn't. Thankfully, our work had become flexible with having them around, and we embraced it. God did so much work, not only in our hearts but others' hearts around us with the children being around. We prayed and fought for this and saw transformation. After a while, we had seen our children's behavior flourish with more of a flow doing ministry as a couple. There wasn't any friction like there had been before due solely to our being intentional about taking those few months away to get things right at home. No child loves to see their parents argue at home, and then put smiley faces on in front of others. There has to be consistency. Do Timothy and I ever fight at home? Of course we do. But this time, we take the time to apologize to our children for our shortcomings and ask them to forgive us. Usually, we are quicker to forgive each other or admit when one of us is wrong because we have discovered that the enemy comes in our minds, telling us to attack each other. This goes the same for parenting. When we are too harsh with the children, we tell them straight away that we are sorry. Humility is key for any family to function well. It's a matter of saying, "I can't do this alone but need God to change me."

Chapter 20

BACK TO AMERICA

As our two kids grew, we thought we were done having children because of my illness and didn't think my body could handle going through pregnancy and lack of sleep again. However, God completely healed me in Australia over the course of the few years. We talked about the possibility of having another one even though our older ones were five and seven, and it seemed a little late to be having another baby. We decided to try again, and lo and behold, a little while later, we were pregnant with a son! Toward the end of our visa in Australia, Timothy led a team to Pakistan, and they preached the gospel there. When he got back, we prayed about direction for our family. We felt the Lord leading us to go back to the states and "get our house in order." We weren't sure at the time what that meant, but in obedience, within a few weeks, we said goodbye to our friends, packed eight suitcases, and said goodbye to the beautiful nation of Australia. Another thing He spoke was we needed to get out of New York.

For fun, I wanted to share our flight story back to America! In the middle of the long flight back to America, my nose immediately got congested from the pregnancy, so I couldn't sleep at all. It is about fourteen hours from Brisbane to LA. On the way to touchdown in California, a few minutes from hitting the ground, the plane shot back up in the air because another plane had to land, causing

Priya to vomit all over herself and the seat. We then landed, found a spare dress for Priya, and took an extra fifteen minutes to change her. Timothy handed me an apple and told me to throw it out, and instead, I ate it but couldn't find a garbage, so I threw the core in our bag. Then we needed to go through immigration and customs and still needed to catch our next flight. But anyone who flies knows that when you fly through LAX, you have to regrab all your checked luggage and scan it through again. Let me remind you, we had eight suitcases, and I was pregnant and tired. The security dog came to our stuff and smelled the apple core. So now we had to scan all of our luggage through again as you're not allowed to bring fruit through, which added another thirty minutes. We also were led to the wrong gates and needed to go through security again and, this time, forgot we had filled water bottles. Now we needed to take a bus to the gate, literally running the whole way, and missed our connection flight by fifteen minutes. We also found out that all flights were full to Tucson for the day, so they put us on a flight to Dallas, then Tucson, which added three more hours to our flight time and was completely out of the way. We got on the flight, and it all of a sudden had tech problems, which we knew we would miss the flight again to Arizona. So we asked to get off the plane and now were back in LAX. All the flights for the day would need to be standby because it was holiday season, and there were four of us. So we waited and knew we would have to stay overnight if we didn't get on one of those flights. Finally, we tried for a flight to Phoenix on standby, and their seats opened up. We quickly decided I'd take it with the kids, and Timothy would stay in LA on standby. After we boarded, a seat opened up on the last LA–Tucson flight for Timothy! Our flights arrived in Tucson within an hour of each other, and we got to the house around 11:00 p.m. Miraculously, we got all of our carry-ons, luggage, and car seats in Tucson.

We spent a week with my sister and then flew to New York right before Christmas. For Christmas, I had an inclination to spend the day with Timothy's dad since he usually spends the holiday alone. We drove out there for a few days, and Timothy had the best father-son conversation that they've ever had, and Timothy's dad said how proud he was of Timothy for following the Lord's call. Around the new year, we started to take a road trip to Texas to try and search for a home base since we hadn't had one since Elijah was born. We made various stops along the way and made it all the way to Houston. Our life drastically changed with an unexpected call that Timothy's dad suddenly passed away. We were both in complete shock because we just had seen him, and he seemed completely fine. We stopped everything we were doing and flew from Texas to New York to organize the wake and funeral. I was six weeks away from giving birth as well. The week we were up in Syracuse just didn't seem real, and Timothy of course was extremely grieved. Thankfully, his brother took his dad's two beautiful Brittany spaniels. Timothy was able to share the gospel in the Catholic church of where the ceremony was. Timothy also was appointed the executor of the estate. So now he would be in charge of pretty much everything going forward. We flew back to Houston to get our car, only to drive it all the way back up to New York. The Lord spoke to us in Australia and told us to go back the states. Had we not, we wouldn't have been able to see Timothy's dad for the last time, and it would have been so much harder to get that news oversees.

Our plans of getting a home were put on hold for a while as we were about to give birth to our son and now had to figure out how to do an estate. Joshua Moses Bulsiewicz was born on March 5, 2020 as a healthy baby, and thankfully, we left the hospital right before COVID started to blow up for the first time. So now, we had a newborn—COVID is a major thing—and we have to start to empty Timothy's dad's house and clean it up to try and sell it in Syracuse, New York. We were living in Saratoga area, New York, which is about two hours east of Syracuse. We gave ourselves about six weeks to adjust with the newborn but then started to work on the house right away. With many trips back and forth, trying to homeschool, sell his dad's possessions, having a new baby, going through the emotional loss of losing a parent, and a lot more, there definitely was plenty of stress for us in 2020. By God's grace, we were not only able to quickly sell his dad's primary home that summer but also his lake home as well that fall. It was definitely a chore emptying out two houses and going through a lot of possessions, but we did it and learned a lot doing it.

By the time the fell hit, we took a few more road trips south, looking at states like Tennessee, South Carolina, and Florida. Timothy felt a pull to make our residency in Florida for 2021, which was very possible because his mom owns another home there, and she was gracious enough to let us live there for the year. We still didn't have any direction on where we should be but continued to take road trips to try and see if the Lord spoke. We felt called to do a two-month Luke 10 school with a ministry called the Last Reformation with Torben Sondergaard. It was a few months in the summer in a city north of Orlando, Florida. We learned so much there about casting out demons, healing, relying on God, living in community, and much more. They had a kids' school while the adults had teaching, so it worked out really well with our kids, and the morning classes happened to be at the same time Joshua took his morning snooze—10:00 a.m. We were also able to take a Luke 10 weekend trip where we went out in teams and didn't take money with us and trusted God to provide meals and lodging for us. We were the only full family in the school that decided to go. It was an amazing trip, and God did so many miracles and went above and beyond, and our faith grew so much!

In the meantime, we are still praying for direction and asking the Lord what is next. After the school, we felt a pull to pioneer and start a non-profit organization called Walking with the Lion. We also had peace about staying in Florida for the next season. As we pray into the vision and mission, we know God will continue to surprise us for the next chapter of our lives in ministry. Our heart still loves third-world nations. But with COVID, we aren't sure what will happen with international travel in the future. We lay that as God's feet and trust that His perfect plan will still prevail as we journey forward with Him.

Chapter 21

Words of Wisdom

John 15 is key. We can't do anything apart from Him. I never really had a revelation of this chapter until I got sick. Like I said before, when I was sick, I couldn't function without God. The average person doesn't need to pray for the strength to take a shower or drive a car safely. John 15:5 says, "I am the vine; you are the branches. If you remain in me and I in you, you will bear much fruit; apart from me you can do nothing." Some things? No! Nothing! It is easy to point at nonbelievers and say that they are walking around like zombies because they are trying to live a life apart from God. Would it be okay to say that believers are doing the same thing? They are going through the motions. They look good on the outside. They appear to be doing great. But what is going on, on the inside? Are they praying? Are they fasting? Are they regularly repenting? Are they pleading with God for Him to be their strength daily? Or are they going to temporary highs, like materialistic things, relationships, food or pleasure, to get by? How easy is it to call a friend when something is wrong instead of going to the scripture? You could say, well, it is wise to get godly counsel—not if we are going to man before God. Who calls their friend who goes to chocolate and reality TV for comfort? Or do we say, "Hey, let's get a group of girls together and do it together"? We could even take it a step further and slander and gossip with a group of Christians and not think anything of it because it is so common in the body of Christ. This is living by the flesh and not living by the Spirit.

Romans 8 is a good model for this. Romans 8:5–8 says, "Those who live according to the flesh have their minds set on what the flesh desires; but those who live in accordance with the Spirit have their minds set on what the Spirit desires. The mind governed by the flesh is death, but the mind governed by the Spirit is life and peace. The mind governed by the flesh is hostile to God; it does not submit to God's law, nor can it do so. Those who are in the realm of the flesh can not please God." It sounds to me that our minds are crucial for this battle between the flesh and the Spirit. It talks about what our minds are set on and governed by. This is a reminder that we *must* renew our minds daily. We cannot afford to take this scripture lightly. Governed means to exercise control over. So if our mind is controlled by fleshly thoughts or desires, it leads us to a life of sin and death. The verse describes that this cannot please God. We need to regularly check our thought life to see if we are in a place where we are thinking on things above, like Colossians describes. If we are not living a life of peace, then our minds are not being governed by the Spirit.

In verse 12, it continues on to say, "Therefore, brothers and sisters, we have an obligation-but it is not to the flesh, to live according to it. For if you live according to the flesh, you will die; but if by the Spirit you put to death the misdeeds of the body, you will live." So again, it reiterates the idea of living by the flesh versus living by the Spirit. One is death, and the other is life. It's not surprising here that there is no gray area. It is one or the other. I believe it would be wise to think about complacency or being lukewarm again and, as I mentioned before, what Jesus said about the church of Laodicea.

There is no hot nor cold. There is either death or life. You're either with Him or against Him. You're a child of God, or you aren't. Do we miss the mark sometimes? Of course, but it should never be an excuse, or we stay in that place of rebellion. As mature believers, if we sin, we should repent, move forward, and never look back. Second Peter 2 is very serious about this as it says, "For if, after they have escaped the pollutions of the world through the knowledge of the Lord and Savior Jesus Christ, they are again entangled in them and overcome, the latter end is worse for them than the beginning. For it would have been better for them not to have known the way of righteousness, than having known *it*, to turn from the holy commandment delivered to them. But it has happened to them according to the true proverb: 'A dog returns to his own vomit,' and, 'a sow, having washed, to her wallowing in the mire.'"

If a sin from the past creeps in again, whether it is a thought of fear or a negative thought toward someone, God reminds me of this verse and gives me this visual picture so that I can be reminded of never going back to sin. It's never a pretty picture picturing you to eat your own vomit, but it drives the point home to never return to old ways or old patterns of sin. We aren't to go near it as it represents disgust, an awful odor, and filth. Why go back to the mud after we have taken a clean shower? It doesn't make any sense at all! One, we have tasted the fresh clean water that only Jesus brings, and two, there is no way that we can be attracted to the mud. If we keep going back to sin, there is something, amiss in our relationship with God. It's a very dangerous place to be, and I've been there too many times to ever want to go back!

We have had the honor to serve at YWAM for just over two years and have learned so much. Timothy was able to travel and minister in Africa, Brazil, and Pakistan in that time, and I was able to in Africa and India. It was eye-opening working with a generation of eighteen- to twenty-five year olds. There are so many amazing things working with this age group—for example, their zeal, passion, and openness. They are away from home for the first time and get to be around other believers they don't know for a half of a year. You aren't only leaving your home nation but also coming into a group of people from many different nations. You realize how similar yet how different you are. In this setting, they are able to be vulnerable and comfortable, sharing their personal testimonies in the first week of class on growing up. Some of which are completely heartbreaking, especially of those who come from Christian homes. They are able to listen to amazing, foundational topics like the Father heart of God, spiritual warfare, and identity. They are eager to learn and have so many questions. There were so many beautiful things I had witnessed—for example, a girl wounded from being raped, and all the males in the class repented on behalf of the person that raped her. We've seen lies break off, and purpose and hope being restored. There are students who were baptized during the school, and their lives got transformed. They also had an outreach phase where they traveled to nations, like India, Africa, Indonesia, Papua New Guinea, and many more, for two months with a team. They were able to be a part of witnessing everything from healings to demonic possessions, getting their hands dirty in humanitarian work.

Being able to travel to a third-world nation for that long really gives you a good sense of missions. Some decide to stay or return to that nation. I believe this was Loren Cunningham's heart to see students go on long-term in missions. In his vision, he saw waves of young people moving out across the continents, announcing the good news of Jesus Christ to the whole earth. He believed that young people didn't need college degrees to share the gospel but only to simply know God and make Him known, which is the statement of YWAM. We were able to work with the DTS, mentor, lead evangelism teams, and just be a support to the base in Australia. What I love most about this age group is the vulnerability and openness. I have found that when we get older, it seems people get more set in their ways and closed off to being open enough to get healing. I believe it's hard to be vulnerable but easier to put on a front in front of people. It's harder for a fifty-year-old pastor to admit he has sinned in his life than a twenty-year-old to say that he is struggling and needs help.

Sometimes, I wonder how people are still shocked when, all of a sudden, some big name in ministry falls away from God and steps down. It shows more of a lack of discernment of those who surround themselves with, "yes, men," and is tied to a people-pleasing spirit. It's rarer that someone admits they are wrong, repents, and seeks counsel. We learned so much in this season as it was our first time in full-time ministry. We were mostly working with young adults. This age can be challenging because of technology and being tied to their phones. It was hard to sit through a three-hour class. I am assuming that university campuses look the same. I know that there have been studies done on social media, technology, and their tie to shortening attention spans. I know, for me personally, I've spent too much time on social media, and it definitely depletes my attention span being in my midthirties. We have chosen to not give the kids iPads or let them watch too much TV for this reason. We encourage them to play outside or be creative in the house. As a homeschooling mom, one could say, "You never have a break. Give yourself one." However, it's not about me at the end of the day, and we feel strongly about this; so we try our best.

Nowadays, it seems the new idea in ministry is having schools. It seems they might be catered more for those in the eighteen- to twenty-five-year-old range because they might have a gap year or choose to take a year off of university to do some kind of ministry school. Although I am in support of doing something like this for a season, I don't think they are the answer to all of life's questions. I believe they can help build one's foundation for sure. But too many times, I've seen a dependency on these schools where they can create a bubble. Students can lean on the organization for a time frame. But when they graduate or come back to normal life, they can tend to fall or struggle. It is key in these schools. We teach them how to keep running the race when trials come or when certain life circumstances happen. I know, for me personally, I grow a lot more through life experiences where it's just God and me than a classroom will ever teach me. This is where I wish we took more time in our lives to fast and intentionally pray. Although I sometimes support counseling or going to friends for advice, I believe that going to God first always is necessary. And then if people confirm what God has already spoken, that is good.

I am guilty of calling a friend before going to God or even seeking advice from my husband about something only God can really answer. I believe God wants us to be dependent on Him to the point where we don't go an hour without praying or thinking about Him. Timothy and I have taken seasons where we fast for a certain period of time for breakthrough or to hear God's voice clearer. Not only does fasting help bring all your weaknesses to the surface, but it points out clearly how much food can be a substitute for God. There have been so many times where I've been stressed and ran straight to caffeine, chocolate, milkshake, or fries to somehow alleviate it. Who goes to a salad or veggies when they are stressed? I, too, have fallen into stress eating before going to God. I think fasting looks different for everybody, but I do believe water-only fasts are the best.

Once, I did a three-day water-only fast, and everything in my body seemed like it was going crazy. However, it did push me into God and became aware of how much things, like caffeine and sugar, had an effect and hold on me. I know people that fast every other day for years and are the kind of people that see revivals in their nations. We are friends with the biggest pastor in Pakistan, and he has told us personally that he and his brother would fast every other day for years, and now there are thousands of Muslims coming to Christ every year, along with miracles, signs, and wonders. There is power in obedience and surrender. And the more dead we are to self, the more He can move through us on His behalf. I don't know enough Christians that fast regularly, let alone even a few times a year. Sometimes we go on social media fasts or fast certain types of food, and that is good. But I really believe we need to push ourselves a bit harder to see breakthroughs and miracles in and around us.

There is a reason why there is a passage in the Bible where the disciples prayed over someone with epilepsy, and he didn't get healed. They didn't see healing and asked Jesus why they weren't healed. He responds, "O faithless and perverse generation, how long shall I be with you? How long shall I bear with you? Bring him here to Me." And Jesus rebuked the demon, and it came out of him and the child was cured from that very hour. Then the disciples came to Jesus privately and said, "Why could we not cast it out?" So Jesus said to them, "Because of your unbelief; for assuredly, I say to you, if you have faith as a mustard seed, you will say to this mountain, 'Move from here to there,' and it will move; and nothing will be impossible for you. However, this kind does not go out except by prayer and fasting" (Matthew 17:17–21).

I believe Jesus is trying to teach something here that fasting is really important, and he rebuked the disciples for their unbelief. Now there were the disciples who had been walking with Him and seeing the miracles left and right, and they had unbelief? We need to take the words seriously when He said, "Faith as a mustard seed," and "Nothing will be impossible for you." I love to tie this in with the scriptures of having faith like a child. Jesus said in Matthew 18:3–4, "Truly I tell you, unless you change and become like little children, you will never enter the kingdom of heaven. Therefore, whoever takes the lowly position of this child is the greatest in the kingdom of heaven."

I've heard the term before, "unbelieving believer." It's funny, but I believe it is so true. There are Christians who doubt more than atheists! We need to look different than the world so that the world is attracted to God in us. We have to be set apart and have faith. After all, this is what true Christianity is all about! We should regularly fast so that we see more of His power in our lives. There are too many scriptures on fasting to list here, but I challenge everybody to study the scriptures on this topic and see that it should never be an after-thought! I believe one of the tactics the enemy uses is complacency within the body of Christ. I think fasting can proactively recognize this and counteract this spirit.

I know when there are times in my life where I am in compla-cency, I or my husband will start a fast. I really believe it's an acceler-ation into His heart. There is a scripture in Isaiah 58:6 that says, "Is this not the fast that I have chose: to loose the bonds of wickedness, to undo the heavy burdens, to let the oppressed go free, and that you break every yoke?" Fasting is also great if there are strongholds pres-ent in one's life. That could be addictions, like pornography, drugs, internet, wine, etc. If there is anything that we go to regularly outside of God, this scripture says this is how to break free of them. So it's not just to see more healing with people we pray for but also for free-dom for ourselves. It is never a formula or based on works.

At times, we can have the wrong motive in fasting and only do it for His hand, not for His heart. God knows our heart. And although fasting can bring us closer in humility, it always goes back to our heart motive in doing it. There have been times where I was doing it out of a work's mentality and trying to earn something from God. I expected His hand because of a formula of fasting for a period of time, but my head was in it more than my heart. It became a burden rather than a joy. And so often, I have caved in when my flesh couldn't do it any longer. This is the whole point, though, to starve the flesh and feed the Spirit. It teaches your body to thrive in hungering more for God than food. Of course, there is wisdom in it too. If you're pregnant, nursing, or having health problems, it might not be the best idea. It's better to be doing some kind of modified fast. But the other side of it is, it can be really good too in detoxing your body and giving your digestive system a break. I believe it can really clear our minds and help us to focus better as long as we keep our eyes fixed on Him through it and not on ourselves.

Most people know this, but we should never fast in hopes to be seen by man or get applause by man either. If we do, we will lose our reward according to Matthew 6:16–18: "And when you fast, do not look gloomy like the hypocrites, for they disfigure their faces that their fasting may be seen by others. Truly, I say to you, they have received their reward. But when you fast, anoint your head and wash your face, that your fasting may not be seen by others but by your Father who is in secret. And your Father who sees in secret will reward you." I think, if you are married, your spouse has to know. But other than that, no one else needs to. Again, it all goes back to heart motive and why we are doing it! God knows. And if we ever tell anyone we are doing it, we need to question the motive behind why we are telling them. I believe, this goes for our giving and other sacrificial acts as well. If we are trying to please man, we will make sure man knows. But if we have a quiet life before God, we will be rewarded by Him. After all, He is our most important audience. We need to understand this because the trap of people-pleasing can be so easy to fall into!

As we get older, we find that life comes in seasons—seasons of busyness, transition, rest, abundance, or lack. In Philippians 4:11–13, Paul gives some good life wisdom: "I am not saying this because I am in need, for I have learned to be content whatever the circumstances. I know what it is to be in need, and I know what it is to have plenty. I have learned the secret of being content in any and every situation, whether well fed or hungry, whether living in plenty or in want. I can do all things through He who gives me strength." Life comes with unexpected situations, whether it is a new baby, a surprise diagnosis, loss of a job, a betrayal from a family member or friend, a location change, or a death of someone near to us. Paul lived in many different circumstances. And don't we as well? We should live a consistent life with fewer trials or tribulations. I think the secret he was talking about in this verse is having intimacy with Christ because He can be the most steady, unchanging thing in our life. We can go through the winds and waves yet have a steady focus where they don't move us.

When I was sick, in the beginning, I was being rocked by every doctor's appointment or symptoms. But the more I would keep my eyes focused on Jesus and renew my mind, the less those things changed me. The Word of God was the only thing that I would allow to go through my mind, and it would steady me. This is so important, especially for women. We tend to be more emotional and sometimes can make decisions based on our emotions or feelings. If you're pregnant, any woman would agree that they could cry at anything or get upset suddenly. We can be more tired and emotional because of hormonal changes going on in the body. I believe with all my heart that there is a place where we can be rock steady as long as our eyes are fixed on Him. There is a place where there is the fruit of the spirit.

> But the fruit of the Spirit is love, joy, peace, forbearance, kindness, goodness, faithfulness, gentleness and self-control. (Galatians 5:22–3)

How amazing would it be if we could exemplify these fruits consistently, no matter what we are going through in life—a tired mom who is not getting enough sleep with a newborn while chasing a toddler who is getting into everything or a father who is working sixty hours per week with a stressful job and little rest. One thing that always needs to be consistent is not budging on our time with the Lord. Never sacrifice that. This is probably one of the most important things to me: to have the character and exemplify this fruit consistently in life. It should be a continual check in our lives. And if we see that we are missing most of these fruits, we need to get back into the presence of our Father. He is perfect and exemplifies these fruits.

So if we spend time with Him, it will be easier to look like Him, and if we look different than the world, the world will be attracted to Christ in us.

This is such a great verse:

> Therefore, rid yourselves of all malice and all deceit, hypocrisy, envy, and slander of every kind. Like newborn babies, crave pure spiritual milk, so that by it you may grow up in your salvation, now that you have tasted that the Lord is good. As you come to him, the living Stone—rejected by humans but chosen by God and precious to him—you also, like living stones, are being built into a spiritual house to be a holy priesthood, offering spiritual sacrifices acceptable to God through Jesus Christ. But you are a chosen people, a royal priesthood, a holy nation, God's special possession, that you may declare the praises of him who called you out of darkness into his wonderful light. (1 Peter 2)

We are to be set apart and look different. If we look like everyone else, why would the world want Jesus? I can't stand to live a double life. It's not okay. We need to be in constant evaluation of ourselves so that we are the salt and light of the earth.

> You are the salt of the earth. But if the salt loses its saltiness, how can it be made salty again? It is no longer good for anything, except to be thrown out and trampled underfoot. You are the light of the world. A town built on a hill cannot be hidden. Neither do people light a lamp and put it under a bowl. Instead they put it on its stand, and it gives light to everyone in the house. In the same way, let your light shine before oth-

ers, that they may see your good deeds and glorify your Father in heaven. (Matthew 5:13–16)

We only get one shot at this life. Let us make it count! On another note, I'm in my midthirties yet embarking on another season of transition!

An important lesson that I have learned in life is that the generations of fear in my family line was, and is, a complete illusion yet was the biggest stumbling block I had between God and I. An illusion is a misinterpreted perception of a sensory experience. It's not real; it's fake. It's like smoke and mirrors. On taking a walk on the beach one day, it appeared as if a storm was coming in, and immediately, fear overwhelmed me. I thought to myself, *Should I cut my walk short because it looks or appears like it was going to storm?* In my spirit, I felt to keep going and not to pay attention to the storm, so I continued to walk and pray. All of a sudden, the storm subsided. Isn't that life sometimes? We focus and base our emotions on what we see and then react based on the seen instead of the unseen. Some people go their entire life this way. If God isn't in our lives, we are living solely according to what we can see and our senses. We were made to live in the unseen realm and move mountains. Let's not fall short of that. Life is an adventure, and it's never too late to let go and let God. We will never regret it!

Endnote

Caroline Leaf, *Switch on Your Brain* (Michigan: Baker books, 2013).

Jonali is a first-generation American whose parents immigrated to the United States from India and also a first-generation Christian from Hinduism. God radically saved Jonali in 2001 and transformed her life by renewing her mind in 2015 while she was fighting for her life with Lyme disease while having a baby and toddler. After she started to recover, she served as a missionary with YWAM (Youth with a Mission) in various nations, such as Australia, Africa, and India with her family. Jonali is a mother and wife currently living in Florida with her husband, Timothy, and three children Elijah John (nine), Priya Mercy (seven), and Joshua Moses (two). Her focus is mothering, homeschooling her children, and managing her household. If she has spare time, she loves to go to a coffee shop and spend time with God or meet with a friend. Her passions are writing, encouraging people through the prophetic, and helping people to practically renew their mind. Ever since she was set free from fear, anxiety, and other mental strongholds, she loves to help those who have struggled with similar battles. For more information, please visit walkingwiththelion.com.